# THE SH!T THEY DON'T TEACH YOU IN SCHOOL:

## A FIELD GUIDE TO GROWTH

—◆—

By
## JUSTIN KORNMANN

Amor Fati Publishing
2024

ISBN: 979-8-218-29973-6

First paperback edition February 2024.

Cover art by Sonny Nicholas

Photographs by David Royer

justinkornmann.com

# Table of Contents

# Introduction

I want to come right out and say this so you don't waste your time wondering, "Who the hell is this guy and why did he write a book about life and personal growth?" I haven't had some rare, fantastical, traumatic event that made me re-examine my life and existence. I'm not a monk or a celebrity or a psychologist. I am, however, an expert on failing, then learning from those failures.

In fact, I still occasionally fail at pretty much everything you will read in the coming chapters. I have not mastered any of it and, to be frank, I don't think anyone truly can because the term "master" tends to be inaccurately defined as "perfection," and none of us are perfect. But I do know that once we become aware of our demons, there's no use fighting them. In the long run, it's just best to befriend them. We can learn from them and use them to help us grow and evolve.

Full disclosure: I initially ended that last sentence, "grow and become better people." But the word "better" seems wrong, as if we aren't good enough right now. "Better" is subjective and can have a negative connotation. But befriending our demons helps us evolve, which doesn't mean perfect, but simply means we are changing and adapting. And that is exactly what I hope we can do together.

This book is based on the friendships I developed with my own demons and the curiosities that were born from them. I'm sharing the tools and lessons that have helped me grow into what I consider to be a more evolved (and much happier) human being.

I firmly believe the goal and purpose of our existence — every day, hour, minute, and second - is to become a more evolved version of ourselves than we were before. We do this by living our lives with more awareness.

To paraphrase life coach Erica Ballard, "We live our lives and heal along the way. We don't heal our lives to live. Life is your teacher." As we go about our daily lives, we heal whenever we bring awareness to the thoughts, feelings, and actions that don't seem to connect with who we are at our core. If these actions are repeated over and over again, they grow into demons that we must face and embrace… or ignore and let them consume us.

Once I stopped fighting my demons and learned to embrace them, I was able to let go and learn from them. I could use them as my compass, my North Star, my GPS. And this written guide you are now reading is what followed.

Throughout your life, anytime you get lost along the way, I hope you can pull out this guide to help you reassess your direction. Most of us are familiar with TV, so I'll use this as an example. TV shows are either serial, meaning each episode takes place after the previous episode for the story to make sense (think Game of Thrones, Breaking Bad, The Sopranos) or they are episodic meaning each episode can stand on its own without needing to reference the previous episodes. (think Law and Order, Big Bang Theory, The Office). This guide is episodic. It was written this way so you can come back to reread any chapter whenever you need a refresh on that specific topic. And, just like the shows listed above, some of these tools may not be for you.

I've intentionally created this guide to help you to find that "more." I'm providing a springboard — a starting point where you can launch your own unique journey of self-growth. The "deep dive" is where you come in.

I recommend, as you make your way through these chapters, that you find your own creative ideas for how you expand and apply each chapter to your unique situation. No amount of words I could ever put down on paper will give you everything you'll ever need. You are the one who can do this work. Rather than me saying more, I encourage you to consider what you can do or say to get the greatest impact from this guide. How can you go deeper? These chapters provide the compass, but you are the one who gets to decide where to go.

Using these tools, I was transformed from someone who had extreme anxiety and frequent depression, to someone who looks forward to waking up each day to learn more about myself and the world around me. I feel connected and grounded. I feel lighter than I have ever felt. And I enjoy the sense of purpose and empowerment that I now feel.

This transformation did not happen overnight. It didn't happen by reading a single book or article, or by listening to a podcast. It happened with time, with patience, with understanding. For some, understanding yourself happens faster than it does for others. For that reason, I hope you will find others on this journey of self-growth so you can help one another. But also, it's still called self-growth for a reason. No one or no thing can force you to make the changes you want to see in yourself or the world around you.

Change comes from within and it only comes with unconditional surrender. I say "surrender" here not to mean "giving up" but rather "giving in" and realizing that you can't control everything. You must know that you will likely fail and that this shit is going to hurt sometimes, but you can and you will bounce back better than ever.

And once unconditional surrender happens, we have to ask ourselves, "Why?" Why do our egos hold onto certain views so tightly? Why is a question you will see again and again throughout this guide. I believe this is one of the most important questions we can ask ourselves.

Now, I'd like to directly ask you a why question. You are here, holding this book in your hands, for a reason that is unique to you. My question isn't, "Why are you here choosing to read this book?" But rather, "Why does growing and evolving even matter to you? What do you hope to get out of this? You may not have the answer now, which is probably why you're reading this book. But I hope this book can help you explore your own whys and bring awareness to the things that will help you evolve into the person you've always wanted to be but didn't know how. You are the reason this book exists.

Here's my why and you can decide if it resonates with you. This path of growth and evolution has so many benefits, but if I had to condense them all into one answer it's this: Peace. For the first time in my life, I began to feel at peace and in control of my own life after literally losing my shit. Peace came when I let go of my attempts to control the outside world and began to focus on understanding what was going on inside of me.

If we can't understand our reactions we won't ever learn to control them and we become slaves to circumstances. Circumstances will always have us by the ovaries and balls. Do you want to live passively and suffer at the hands of fate? Or would you like to live proactively and turn whatever fate throws your way into literally the adventure of a lifetime?

Ever have that feeling that something is missing, but you can't quite put a finger on what it is? We all have that feeling at times, which is probably what brings most people to self-help and self-improvement. But that thing makes it difficult to get a handle on life. Events "never go our way" and tiny problems turn into "horrific" experiences. These feelings are all results of not being in control of the outside world and thinking that we need to be.

No one will ever hand you the reins of fate. You must steer yourself with the wind you create through your actions. This is the way to inner peace. And when you're on this path, everything else seems to fall into place more easily.

For control freaks like myself, this task can seem daunting. But just as it is futile to swim against the currents of the ocean, it is a hopeless battle to fight the currents of life. The only way to find peace is to let go and accept that the only thing you control is how you respond to life.

If you choose to go on this journey with me and accept these terms, I firmly believe the following chapters can impact you for the rest of your life.

There will be situations that will make these lessons more difficult to apply. This is natural. There will be times when you want to give up. This is understandable. There will be times when you think that you have made progress only to have devastating setbacks. This is inevitable.

How do I know this? Because it has and still does happen to me and everyone who has embarked on this adventure before me. We must not give up. We must walk down this path, and when obstacles come, we should not only face them, but also enjoy the process of conquering them so we can continue forward. This is the path we must take to become a more enlightened people and society.

It starts with you. It starts from within. And, if we are all working on ourselves, that means the world is on its way to becoming a better place.

## TIPS:

Welcome to the tip section. At the end of every chapter, you will find a section that may contain exercises you can try, books, articles, or other resources that I've found helpful. I caution you to not overwhelm yourself by implementing all the tips at once. I suggest you tackle the most pertinent to yourself and once you feel you have a handle, move on to the next. Remember, growth is a life-long game, so implement one section of tips for let's say, a month or whatever timeframe works best for you, then expand to the next area of your life that requires focus and build from there. Just like everything else in this book, some of the tips may not be for you. We each have our own path to travel. If none of these tips work for you, brainstorm your own ideas. We should question everything, which includes everything you read in this book. Come to your own conclusions and decide what's best for you.

# PART I:
# Accept

# 1.
# Choose to Change

————◆————

*"The most successful jihad is the conquest of one's self."*

**- Prophet Muhammed**

(peace be upon him)

This is going to be very shocking to some of my family and friends who will read this. I was a smoker for over fifteen years. Yep, I was a closet smoker. Sorry, Mom and Dad. I started back when I was 18 and I'd smoke a few cigarettes here and there. But the few cigarettes turned into smoking more than a few and on a regular occurrence. I told myself I could quit whenever I wanted and that it was no big deal.

If it was no big deal, why did I hide it from so many people? Why did I even do it in the first place? It was a coping mechanism. It was how I dealt with life because it's how I thought life was. I thought everyone felt depressed and down and that we all needed to have guilty pleasures to survive it. And deep down I knew I was doing it because it was a way to slowly kill myself. It was a way to end the pain that I was living in.

I wasn't happy. I didn't know what I wanted or who I was. I felt lonely and I felt helpless and cigarettes were a dignified way out. I put on my smile and went out into the world and was the fun person I was always expected to be. Sure, I did have actual good days, but something always felt off. I couldn't pinpoint it and I didn't even try to investigate it. It was too painful.

But you can only hide your pain and your bad habits for so long. The mask that you wear may hide you from the outside world, but you can't hide from yourself. You can either pick up that pack and light another or you can choose the more difficult alternative to change by acknowledging that you just aren't happy and that this isn't the only way to get through life.

You can and should have support from others. But this is the one area where no one else can help you, but you. Not me, not your mom, or anyone else on this planet. It's got to be your choice. And the beauty of it is that you can make that moment happen whenever you want.

For me, that moment happened in May of 2018. I was going through a rough patch in my life. I had just completed a movie I produced and I was waiting for it to be released. I had done the work and then had nothing but time on my hands. I didn't have a task or job or anything else to focus on that gave me a sense of purpose. I had all of this energy but nowhere to put it.

So, I put that energy into a relationship that was never meant to be and I knew it. I chose to ignore the red flags because this relationship had become my next "project". Needless to say this "project" wasn't going as planned. Pair that with the fact that I had no idea how the movie would do or what my next film would be and I became an anxiety-filled dumpster fire of a person who was on the fast-track toward a breakdown.

I first decided to cope with the stress by hanging out with my friends, getting drunk, and numbing the pain away. But that didn't work. I lost weight, I lost my appetite, I lost who I was as a person. All I did was drink, smoke cigarettes, and torture myself with a woman I knew wasn't right for me. I was exhausted and unhappy. I knew I needed a change when my family and friends noticed the dramatic difference in my behavior. Their concerns pushed me to look further at myself and my situation.

I decided it was time to reach out for help. So I made an appointment with my doctor, who prescribed me antidepressants and referred me to a therapist. Thankfully, I was able to see that therapist the next day. In my case, seeing a therapist was enough and I never needed to take medication. (This is just my scenario, you have to decide what's best for you.) I needed a change in how I approached life. I needed to make different choices than I had in the past. I needed to face my demons rather than hiding from them.

I delved into learning as much as I could. I read countless books on growth, relationships, stoicism, breathing, meditating, you name it. If it was something I found interesting and thought I could benefit from, I read it.

Not only did I read, I applied that knowledge and began to carefully observe myself. Through journaling, reflection, and asking myself some tough questions, I was able to get out of that funk. That process set me on a new path.

It all started with the decision to not numb the pain away, but to lean into it and do the hard work of asking *why*? Why do I feel this way? Why do I think this way? Why am I so unhappy with my life? What do I want out of life? How can I use my gifts for the betterment of the world?

Choosing to change led me to realize that I was living by the belief that in order to be happy I needed success, someone to love, and for that person to love me in return. I also discovered that, before any of those things became possible, I first needed to start loving myself. I had to decide to change out of love for myself and for no other reason.

None of us will change if we are doing it for someone else. We'll never change to reach some materialistic goal. It all starts with the love we have for ourselves.

We can't evolve as people if we are under the false assumption that we are perfect. Or by simply ignoring our faults. Eventually, we learn the inevitable truth that we are not perfect nor are we broken.

Society has taught many of us that any admission of imperfection is a sign of weakness. We see the perfect models, the perfect meals, the perfect angle of every photo on social media. We think we need to embody that perfection. But the models and meals are just what we see in the frame, not the whole picture.

We don't see the life of the model behind the scenes at their job. We don't see how they sometimes struggle to get out of bed for a photoshoot. They have difficulties with their relationships and career goals. They have days when they, too, question their existence in the world.

That perfect meal that you're salivating over may not even be real. It could be a prop made out of plastic because someone wanted the perfect look to "capture the moment." And, even if the food is real, just remember that it started out just like the food you see at the grocery store. It's raw meat, veggies, or other ingredients that are thoughtfully combined, seasoned and cooked. Why couldn't you make a meal just like that with practice? Then, when you go buy the food and make it, you can feel proud because you changed it into something you desire. *That* is how you create your reality. You do it for yourself--for your own satisfaction--not for likes on social media.

Reality is knowing that things are always changing and that none of us are an exception to this reality. We are always evolving, but *how* we grow and experience change is up to us. We can evolve solely as the result of outside forces, such as technological innovations and changes in society or we can expand internally based on the person we want to become.

Ancient Greek philosopher Epictetus taught that every situation has two handles: "One of the handles will hold weight, the other won't." Are you going to grab the one that empowers you? Or the one that destroys you? The one that destroys you will be the never-ending cycle of your own bad habits. Failing to break those habits and ignoring the opportunities to change creates a deep hole that gets harder and harder to climb out of. You may climb a few feet, you may even see the surface from time to time, but until you discover why you're stuck in that hole, you will be unable to reach ground level.

Breaking self-destructive habits means choosing to do the hard and often painful work of questioning the *why* behind your actions and feelings. Facing them head on is the only way forward. And the time to do that is often when you're faced with challenges. Most people don't decide to make changes when they're riding high unless something still feels off.

The times when you feel the most lost are the times when you are most likely to be found. But only *you* can find *yourself*. Only *you* can be the one who chooses to change.

## TIPS:

Start a journal. Write in it every day. It doesn't matter what you write, but just get in the habit of writing something. Here are some questions you might want to start with: Why are you choosing to expand as a person? What brought you here? What do you want to get out of reading this book? What do you want to get out of life? What is it about yourself that you would like to change? I'm not talking about being taller, thinner, wittier... I'm talking about you as a person.

Once you choose to change, it's not happening overnight and it's definitely not happening without your full attention and commitment. So starting a journal will help you honor that commitment to your growth and it will strengthen your ability to reflect and process things that come up for you.

**Resources:**

*The Daily Stoic Journal* by Ryan Holiday and Stephen Hanselman

# 2.
# Be Uncomfortable, Be Vulnerable

*"Vulnerability is not winning or losing; it's having the courage to show up and be seen when we have no control over the outcome. Vulnerability is not weakness; it's our greatest measure of courage."*

**- Brené Brown**

Have you ever gone bowling? If so, how was your first attempt? Often when someone first learns how to bowl, bumpers are set up to keep the ball from going into the gutters. Bumpers remove any chance that you won't hit a pin on your first bowl.

I think bumpers are absolute shit. I believe we need to remove the bumpers. We need to roll that ball into the gutter in order to become better bowlers. And you know what? You'll get another go at it because that ball always comes back. You'll get better with every single roll. And you will continue to get more rolls until the game is over or until you decide to quit. If you keep those bumpers up you'll never be ready for the real game. You'll be accustomed to "training wheels" and you won't know how to react. In fact, you won't even be playing the same game.

The same is true in life. Putting yourself in situations where you are uncomfortable and might fail is the only way to grow. Think about your life right now. If you never change anything and never expand your horizons, your life will remain the same. If you are okay with that and you're happy where you're at, that's amazing! But is there really no room for improvement? Most of us have room to evolve and grow our skillsets. Why not give it a go and put yourself in situations that you aren't accustomed to?

The first time I really did this was when I took my first solo trip and spent more than five weeks in Peru. It was one of the best experiences of my life. I met so many amazing people from around the world. The Peruvian people were welcoming and proud to share their history, their cities, and their way of living. I hiked to Machu Picchu, I zip-lined over the rainforest, rode buggies in the desert, and did an ayahuasca ceremony with two people I had just met who are now friends for life. I did all this without knowing much Spanish in a foreign country thousands of miles away from anyone I knew. And it was fan-fucking-tastic.

After I returned back to the States, I wondered exactly what made that trip so life-changing. Yes, the culture, the food, the people, all of it was truly spectacular, but I have amazing friends where I live. I have great food options and a really cool city with plenty of culture. So what was the difference?

The difference is that I did everything out there on my own. I never knew what I was getting myself into. I took chances and I was out of my element. The short answer: I got uncomfortable. I had become complacent and wasn't challenging myself. I was just going through my routine and skating by. I had a steady job, good friends, and a comfortable life.

I believe traveling is beneficial for so many reasons and something most everyone can do, because it really offers new perspectives of the world. Doing it alone can be scary. You are by yourself in a place that is unfamiliar to you. You are forced to adapt. You are forced to connect with others. You are forced to ask questions to get by.

But discomfort can bring immense joy to life because it's an obstacle to overcome. It's a way to expand our lives. I knew I needed to not only *embrace* the discomfort, but to *seek* it.

Thankfully for me, fate led me to a methodology that revolves around getting uncomfortable and pushing your boundaries. I first encountered The Wim Hof Method after reading James Nestor's book, *Breath*. If you don't know who Wim Hof is, I will provide some information in the tip section at the end of this chapter because he is someone worth getting to know. He has climbed to the death zone of Everest without oxygen while wearing nothing but shorts and hiking boots. He ran a marathon in the Namib Desert without drinking water, and he has demonstrated how we can influence our autonomic nervous system, in turn activating our immune system, voluntarily. And he developed his method while dealing with the tragic death of his first wife. The Wim Hof Method revolves around breath work, cold exposure, and mindset. I won't go into full detail on this here, even though I desperately want to. But for the purpose of this field guide, what you need to know for now is that his method revolves around hormesis, or mild environmental stress that has a positive impact on our bodies and minds.

A physical example of hormesis is working out. Lifting weights or going on a run puts stress on your muscles initially, then your muscles recover and come back stronger. Our brain responds to stress like a muscle too, it's just easier to see progress through physical activities. We can see our time improve on a run, increase the amount of weight we can lift or raise the number of pushups when we are becoming physically stronger. But it's more challenging to see the progress we make with our minds.

How do we progress through hormesis mentally? We work out our minds by getting uncomfortable. We push ourselves through mental and physical challenges. When we're fatigued and attempt to do one more pushup, it is the mind helping us push past the physical discomfort.

If you give a presentation in front of your coworkers that you're terrified to give, you're using your mind to push past the nerves. You make yourself temporarily uncomfortable to become stronger in the long run, all the while training your mind to know that you can do more than you think you are capable of.

The more we live in the discomfort, the more of it we can tolerate. We expand all of our muscles, including the one between our ears. As Wim Hof says, "The limit is not the sky, the limit is the mind."

Here's an example. Juan Pujol Garcia was a Spanish spy and double agent in WWII. But before that he was unsuccessful in nearly every endeavor he attempted. He was a failed student, businessman, soldier and even tried dabbling in cinema. All of that didn't deter him from reaching out to the British Army to work with them against the Nazis. Once again though, he failed at this attempt. The British turned him away, so he approached the Nazis to spy on the Allies for them. He was accepted by the Nazis and after he gained their confidence, he went back to the Allies to work as a double agent. They finally accepted his offer.

Juan began feeding the Nazis misinformation and even convinced them that he had a network of nearly 30 other spies working with him that needed funding. His misinformation cost them millions of wasted dollars and he was crucial in convincing the Nazis that the D-Day attacks were just a diversion. The Nazis never caught on. In fact, he was so trusted by the Nazis that he even received an Iron Cross medal, a medal that required Hitler's approval. Can you imagine how terrified he must have been, knowing that getting caught would have resulted in certain death?

Though he was never caught, Garcia was so scared for his life after the war was over that he faked his own death so he could live his life in peace without having to look over his shoulder for disgruntled Nazis. Juan Pujol Garcia accomplished these amazing feats despite constant rejection. He stepped into the unknown and most certainly got uncomfortable. He was able to succeed because he made himself vulnerable, again and again. His willingness to push the limits of his mind and risk it all helped change the course of history.

It's time to take off the sweatpants and try on some skinny jeans. Yes, I'm looking at you. To make change happen in your life, and to evolve into the person you want to become, it's going to take work. And that work is going to get uncomfortable. You're going to feel vulnerable just like Juan, and you need to be prepared to fall flat on your face. The greatest accomplishments that ever occur come from people stepping out of their comfort zone and going into the unknown. Discoveries become discoveries because no one else has dared to make that venture. Without people risking failure or, in Juan's case, risking death, nothing new would ever happen. We'd still be traveling by foot because no one would have dared to hop up on a horse. So why would it be any different for our self-growth and becoming more evolved versions of ourselves?

People don't change for many reasons--they think it's too hard, or too scary, or they're afraid of losing friends. Bottom line: it's uncomfortable to travel into the unknown. When we get comfortable in our daily lives, even if we don't enjoy our days that much, somehow the unknown seems worse. But I ask you, if you are already unhappy, how much more unhappy can the unknown make you? Isn't it worth the risk of finding happiness in the unknown rather than staying unhappy in your current situation?

Now, don't get me wrong, it's not all sunshine, lollipops, and rainbows. You are going to fail sometimes. You are going to look and sound like a jackass from time-to-time. But is that really any different from your daily life? I can't think of anyone who has ever graced this planet who hasn't screwed up and looked like an idiot every now and then.

You don't have to jump off the deep end and forever abandon safe waters. Boyd Varty says in his book, *The Lion Tracker's*

*Guide to Life,* "Too much uncertainty is chaos, but too little is death." Find balance, but you must take risks.

In order to take that step toward progress, do things that scare you. Maybe you need to quit the job you hate. You'll need to ask your crush out for dinner. Or tell your parents you aren't going to medical school because you want to be a fashion designer. It doesn't all have be extreme. You can start with baby-steps, like switching up your daily routine, trying a new cuisine, or volunteering at a non-profit you've been interested in but were too scared to go by yourself.

You will need to take risks and chances, both externally and internally. You'll start leading with who you are at your core rather than simply following societal norms. You may lose friends and you may completely change your lifestyle. Things will get uncomfortable, but it's okay. This is what has to happen in order to improve yourself and your life.

Tim Ferriss has an uncomfortable challenge in his book, *The 4-Hour Workweek.* He suggests that you lie on the ground in public for ten seconds. People will look at you funny. They may laugh. They may point. But you are taking a risk. And by taking a risk like that, you are being vulnerable. The more you step out of your comfort zone, you'll have less of a problem doing other things that make you uncomfortable.

Building up the courage to take risks requires practice.

If you start by doing silly, obscure things with no real repercussions, then you'll build up the thicker skin needed to take on the larger risks that come with internal growth. Then, once you stop caring what the outside world thinks of you, the more confident you'll become with who you are. The more confident you become *internally*, the more willing you are to be uncomfortable with your *external* growth.

Your internal growth feeds your external growth. But no growth comes from playing it safe. If you want views from the mountain top, you'll have to leave the comfort of your house.

## TIPS:

If you're not into the Tim Ferriss uncomfortable challenge, start with this: Once a month give up something different that you enjoy doing. Maybe it's alcohol, or chocolate, or caffeine? It doesn't matter what it is as long it's a thing of comfort to you. Don't worry, you can reintroduce your guilty pleasures the next month, but challenge yourself.

It also doesn't hurt to ask yourself why you enjoy that thing so much. Why does it bring you comfort? There are no right or wrong answers, but it is good to be aware.

There is a great app I used to stop smoking called, *Craving to Quit.* It was created by neuroscientist Dr. Jud Brewer who has a wonderful TED Talk about mindfulness and how we some-times develop our habits through false narratives. For example, you don't smoke to relieve stress, but you smoke when you are stressed. If you really begin to taste and feel what you are doing, you begin to see that this isn't something you enjoy doing. This same mindset can be applied to just about anything. I highly recommend the app. And to find more information on the pro-cess itself, watch his TED Talk. (Now, I kind of feel like I'm a walking advertisement for TED Talk.)

I also recommend doing things alone, like going to a random meet-up group by yourself, taking a free city tour of your own city, or traveling. Traveling is one of the best ways to grow. It forces you to take the lessons you are learning in life and to apply them. It puts you into the most uncomfortable but thrilling of situations.

If you think traveling is too expensive or you don't know where to start, I get it. I thought the same thing, and it always kept me from taking that leap. I ended up booking a trip through my friend, Alex, who started her own travel design company. At the time this was written, Alex has been to all seven continents and to more than 50 countries. She did all of this traveling while she was making less than $30,000 per year!

Yes, if she can do it and I could do it, so can you. Here is a link to her website if you want to get started on your adventure: GoAwayAlexTravel.com

If that is out of your price range, travel doesn't have to mean far-off distances, either. If you live in the city, head out to the country. If you live in the country, venture into the city. Put yourself in a different atmosphere, that's what it's all about. Get uncomfortable and prove to yourself that you can navigate through unfamiliar terrain.

**Resources:**

*Daring Greatly* by Brené Brown

*The 4-hour Workweek* by Tim Ferris

Craving to Quit App

# 3.
# There is No Happiness Without Suffering

———◆———

*"Happiness is possible, right now, today. But there is no happiness without suffering."*

**- Thich Nhat Hanh**

When you first start out on this journey of self-discovery it can be fucking ugly. At least it was for me. I noticed all of my flaws in the worst possible ways and they made me cringe.

There's no need to avoid these feelings, and you absolutely do not want to beat yourself up over them. Acknowledge them. Study them. And ask, "Why do I feel this way?"

So often when we experience thoughts and feelings that we don't enjoy, we either wallow in our disappointment with ourselves, or we completely ignore them and live in denial. When we wallow in those feelings, it's easy to beat ourselves up. We might feel as if there is something wrong with us and might even think of ourselves as inferior to others. Then come the regrets... "If I had only done this," or "If I'd just said that," I wouldn't be so sad, angry, or humiliated.

The truth is, all of these feelings are completely natural and of the utmost importance. If we didn't experience sadness, how would we know what joy feels like? One cannot exist without the other. You have to have the yin to have the yang because they are two sides of the same coin.

We all feel these emotions. There is nothing wrong with you when you're feeling down. We all ride the rollercoaster of emotional ups and downs. I believe that becoming a "positive" society to the extreme, with the expectation that we should always be "happy" is unhealthy. It is impossible to maintain that same level of happiness all the time. Something always feels better or worse than something else.

While being positive and looking at the glass half-full is great, there's no need to feel inferior for having an off day or for being sad for no other reason than that you feel fucking sad. It's so easy to compare different emotions and decide that some are better than others, but are they *really*? We may need to feel sadness in order to move on from heartache or loss. Overlooking sadness or forcing ourselves to be happy doesn't get rid of the sadness, but suppresses it. Then it builds and builds and builds. So let's stop comparing emotions to one another and just set them free.

We also tend to compare our emotional state of being with how we perceive other people are doing. We sure do love to compare, don't we? When we compare ourselves to others, this can go one of two ways. Either we can conclude that we aren't like anyone else because we think we are better--more superior--or we might believe we aren't like anyone else because we are inferior. I hate to break it to you but, once again, this isn't an either/or scenario.

Avoiding certain feelings is typically an attempt to suppress them, in the hopes that they'll go away if we can just think about something else. We drown them out with mind-numbing activities, such as binging TV, stuffing our faces with junk food, or losing ourselves in alcohol and drugs. We think that these are ways to deal with problems because that's what society and the ever-powerful marketing forces tell us.

The toxic "solutions" we indulge in might temporarily make us feel better, but actually feed the beast from within. Those feelings will come back. And they will come back with a vengeance because they've been pent up inside us. Then, the slightest irritation can set us off. Even something as small as the guy who accidentally bumps into you in the grocery line, the comedown after a big social event, or that one friend who hasn't texted you back yet. These could all be tiny sparks that ignite suppressed feelings and create huge flames.

So often, in our daily thoughts or even in meditation, we not only judge these feelings, but we judge ourselves. We can even feel as if we *are* our emotions. Acknowledging negative feelings but from a place of love helps us recognize that our emotions are <u>not</u> us. They are simply the result of how we feel about an occurrence, or in Buddhist terms, *the object*.

Sayadaw Tejaniya recommends in his book, *When Awareness Becomes Natural,* asking yourself what kind of thoughts are in your mind and what is your attitude towards them? How do you feel about each thought? Answer that question to yourself, then ask what is the reason for that thought? What is driving it? When you've answered that question to yourself, consider what you are feeling, not just emotionally, but physically? By answering each question, we are able to get to the root of our defilements, which is what Buddhists call "unwholesome actions that can cloud the mind." The most common defilements are anxiety, jealously, fear, anger, desire, and depression, and each of them can really get a hold of us and destroy us from inside.

Getting to the root of our defilements helps us look at our thoughts and feelings with curiosity--more like investigators rather than judges, juries and executioners. When we investigate without judgement, we can observe what is going on inside us and see more clearly that it is not our identity. When we observe anger in ourselves, we don't need to say, "I am angry" because we are not actually anger itself. We are "feeling angry."

I know, I know. When I first heard this I thought, "Okay, hippie. Whatever you say," with an eye roll. But it works.

You are so much more than a feeling. If you "are angry" then you would be incapable of feeling anything but anger, ever. Those who stay on the path of identifying as anger may just get their wish.

The human mind has a difficult time separating our identity from a feeling when we say we *are* this emotion. For instance, when you *feel* angry and you keep saying that you *are* angry, you recondition yourself to be angry more and more often.

It is important to feel emotions, but it is just as important to not let them rule you. We've all met the hothead, the drama queen/king, the Negative Neds and Nancys. These are the people who let their emotions rule them rather than dealing with those thoughts and feelings head on. They lean into the emotion so hard that they make it their identity without ever dealing with the root cause. Some people get stuck in this mindset or, in some cases, might crave the attention they receive from that emotion. You can change this pattern by recognizing it, asking yourself why you feel this emotion, and investigating what causes it to reappear over and over again. In time, you will begin to see what is happening, not just in your mind but in your body.

Because our minds and bodies are so connected, we sometimes incorrectly attribute certain physical reactions to something we must have "tweaked". But, in reality, our bodies are always giving us warning signs when something is going on inside the mind.

A racing mind can become so common for many of us that we assume this is normal. We get accustomed to letting thoughts and emotions fester and control us, fighting them rather than accepting them. But when we fight, we cause stress in our resistance, which can eventually cause us to break. This kind of physical and emotional break is what forced me to find another way to cope with life.

Listen to your body and see what is going on in your mind. You may feel off, but you're not sure what it is. You might feel blah, but you can't explain it. This happens when you aren't paying attention to the connection between your mind and your body.

Your brain and body are connected through neural pathways made of neurotransmitters, chemicals, and hormones. These pathways are always transmitting signals between your brain and your body, and control our breathing, our digestion, and even signals to us when we feel pain and pleasure. Even when we know our mind and body are connected in this manner, why do we overlook the connection the body has to our emotions and vice versa?

Listening to your body is the first sign that something is shifting within your mind. The body is the signal flare to start the evaluation process. Listen to it. Connect with it. Discover how it is connected to each feeling you are experiencing.

Watch for patterns. For example, often when you need to say something difficult to someone or you aren't speaking your truth, your throat will hurt. Or when you feel sad and anxious, you may get upset feelings in your stomach or you lose your appetite. When you're stressed out, your blood pressure rises or you may develop ulcers. We've all felt physical pains before and too often we just overlook what they might be telling us. Multiple studies show how feeling down and depressed can weakened the immune system and cause chronic inflammation.

Start to notice your physical feelings and see how they relate to what's going on in your mind. You may not need a pain pill for your physical body, but instead you might just need a good cry, an honest conversation, or to beat the shit out of your pillow. Your mind and your body are not two separate entities, but they are so intertwined that they're inseparable.

When you see for yourself how the mind and body are one in the same, you can begin to find answers in places you never knew to look. The more you can decipher your feelings, the more you can understand yourself. And the more you understand yourself, the more growth can occur.

Pain is inevitable. You can't grow without growing pains. But when you know what to do with it, you are finally able to let the pain teach and guide you forward.

# TIPS:

Be kind to yourself when you are self-evaluating. Don't call yourself any names or think about how you "should" be. Treat yourself like you're talking to your best friend. Be kind, be gentle, but be honest.

Ask yourself what kinds of thoughts are in your mind and what is your attitude towards each of those thoughts? How do you feel about that thought? What is driving it? What are you feeling, not just emotionally, but physically?

**Resources:**

*When the Body Says No: The Cost of Hidden Stress,* by Gabor Maté

*When Awareness Becomes Natural: A Guide to Cultivating Mindfulness in Everyday Life,* by Sayadaw Tejaniya

# 4.
# Life *is* Unfair

————•••◆•••————

*"Our life is what our thoughts make it."*

**- Marcus Aurelius**

Life is unfair. But its unfairness has no bias. In Jay Shetty's *Think like a Monk,* one of his teachers tells students, "Think about a time in life that something occurred to you that you didn't deserve." So stop reading and do that right now.

OK, what was it? I bet it was a time when something you perceived as a negative occurrence happened to you? That's because we are all conditioned to have a negative bias, mostly due to our biological design for survival and our societal influences that trigger it. It's part of our DNA, our fight or flight response.

Throughout the course of human history we weren't always the predators we are now. We used to spend our time in nature where we had to be on constant alert of threats. A bear or wolf could attack our campsite at a moment's notice. A rainstorm could wash a mountain down on us. Long before the evolution of mankind, animals, and yes we are animals too, have had to react to perceived harmful events, attacks or threats to survival. So naturally, we are more stimulated by perceived negative occurrences than we are by positive circumstances.

This is why negative news coverage happens almost 24/7 while good news is found primarily on niche platforms. Negativity surrounds us on social media as well. What drives the clicks is news that scares us. Television and movies often have the threat of some evil approaching, whether it be a living being of some sort, or an act of nature. Conflict (and usually overcoming that conflict) is the driving force in every single form of entertainment. Just as sex sells, so does drama. Not a lot of people would really enjoy watching the perfect life unfold. It would be boring because it doesn't trigger our "spidey" senses for survival.

Unfortunately, news outlets care more about their advertising dollars than showing a balanced news cycle and entertainment executives are all about the bottom line. There are so many good people doing good things that surround us, but mostly what we see and hear about are the murders, corruption, and despair in the world.

We are actually living in the most peaceful time of recorded history, but we all feel like we are in the biggest shitstorm that has ever graced the earth. Are bad things happening? Yes, absolutely, but not more than other times in history. Thanks to technology, we not only get to read about it all, but we can see it in high-definition footage. Yet we don't have to let the negative bias of our surroundings affect our outlook or allow it to defeat us.

The next time something bad happens to you that you didn't deserve, remind yourself of a time when something good happened to you that you didn't deserve. Remember that time when a restaurant accidentally gave you an extra chicken tender, or when you were running late and that car just so happened to pull out of a front row spot just as you were pulling in? Once you start remembering all of the good you didn't deserve, you'll notice a change in thought. You'll stop thinking you deserve an outcome and realize the outcome is just the outcome.

Both the conveniences and inconveniences life throws your way are assisting you in some capacity. As soon as you let go and accept that life is also unfair in your favor you will see that you are not a victim of its wrath. This realization can help you accept your circumstances and even become grateful for whatever comes your way.

Expectations fuck us up. When we have expectations outside of our control, we are either shocked by the result because we never thought this outcome was possible or we get the result we wanted but aren't grateful for the outcome because we expected that this is how it should always be. Expectations are usually unrealistic, either because the end results aren't what we dreamed they would be or, in some cases, things didn't happen the way we thought they would occur even if the result was what we hoped for.

My experiences have taught me to care more about training and preparation than outcomes. I now place more emphasis on what I control--*my* actions. And I highly recommend this shift for anyone and everyone. If we prepare *ourselves* then we are ready for whatever outcome may come our way.

I get it, this is easy to say and hard to actually do. But the only way this shift will get easier is to practice it, day in and day out. To be clear, I am *not* saying that you shouldn't have ambitions in life. I *am* saying to do everything in your control to make a difference knowing that the rest is out of your hands.

Rather than setting expectations about the outcome of things, shift your focus to the standards you set for yourself. If you want that job, put yourself out there. Send those e-mails and make those phone calls. Practice for the interview and knock it out of the park. Then, get it out of your head and move on. You did your job. You prepared. You hustled. But the end result? That's not a part of your process. That's the boss's call or whoever the hell is in charge of the final decision. It's not yours. Other candidates did the same thing for this role, but it will only go to one person. No matter the outcome, it's going to be "unfair" somehow. So work your ass off. Know that your time and effort is its own reward, and that is the part of life you control.

## TIPS:

Practice gratitude. One of the biggest ways to get yourself out of a bad mood and to realize that you aren't a victim is to be grateful for the things you have.

Every morning, write down three things you are grateful for. A roof over your head, a job, even the two-dollar ramen noodle in your cabinet. Be grateful for it all.

Something I find helpful in regards to gratitude are thank you notes. Thank you notes help you reflect on how individuals have impacted your life. So write a letter to a friend, family member, or someone you just met who provided you with an act of kindness. By sending them a thank you card, you are re-minded of how lucky you are to have encountered these people and they will feel the love you felt by their kindness.

So often, we think people know how we feel about them and we allow things to go unsaid. In our busy lives, it's easy to forget to take the time to show appreciation. We get caught up in the hustle and bustle. And the next thing we know it's too late to tell that someone what they mean to us. Don't make that mistake. It's a task that takes very little effort and has a tremendous impact on you and the recipient.

There are a couple social media accounts who post just uplifting content. I follow these accounts and turn to them when I'm feeling overwhelmed with negativity. Find those accounts below.

**Resources:**

*Think Like a Monk,* by Jay Shetty

@tanksgoodnews

@goodnews_movement

# 5.
# Perception is Everything



*"There is nothing good or bad, but thinking makes it so."*

**- William Shakespeare**

Once we realize we don't have control over what life throws at us and the only thing we have control over is how we react, then nothing good or bad ever happens. "Good" and "bad" are just our perspectives of these circumstances. You're late for a meeting because the power went out and your alarm didn't go off. You forget your coffee at home and now you're stuck in traffic. You can either get angry about these situations or learn from them. Set up a backup alarm, start getting up earlier, stop relying on coffee to "wake you up." Okay, okay, maybe that last part about the coffee is extreme, but you get the point.

Take a situation...*any* situation...and use it to your advantage. What can you take away that could help you grow into a more evolved person? Can you think of a time when life threw you a curve ball and you were still able to get on base, and maybe even score? What did that accomplishment feel like? I know for me, it feels pretty damn good.

In 2003, I left college after my first semester and decided to move out to Los Angeles to pursue my dream of working in the film industry. I hopped on my flight, flew to LA, and found an apartment. I was all set. But there was an issue with my plan. I was still smitten with my high school crush who lived in Wisconsin. We had ended our long-distance relationship before I moved, but we still talked often and I still had feelings for her. I also wanted to play soccer in college as I missed the game, the structure of training, and the competition it offered.

After being in LA for no longer than one day, I began having reservations. I kept thinking about Wisconsin and began wondering if maybe I should move to Wisconsin, walk-on to a team and play soccer, and see where life would take me.

I've never wanted to be someone who wonders years down the road what might have been. So I chose the most uncomfortable thing I could have possibly imagined at that point and followed my gut instinct. I left LA after only living there one day. I probably still hold the record for the shortest living stint of anyone who ever moved to LA.

I'd be lying if I didn't tell you that I was embarrassed to make that choice. I had just said my goodbyes to all of my friends and family. The thought, "Oh my god, what is my dad going to think?" weighed heavily on my mind. My dad is a highly logical person and this was not a logical move. Though I didn't want my parents to be disappointed in me, I was at peace. It felt like the right decision. And it may have looked crazy to others but, to this day I still feel like I made one of the most sane decisions I could have made. I wasn't influenced by anything or anyone else. I did what I felt I needed to do. I trusted my intuition against all else.

I moved in with my great-aunt and uncle, who had a farm. I found a job working at a mortgage company and got situated into a routine there. I met friends, some I knew from the past and others were new acquaintances, and I spent a lot of time with my cousin, who was in college, and I even survived a Wisconsin winter.

I was able to see the relationship with my high school crush wasn't doomed by the distance, we were just incompatible. We would always have a special connection, but we were just two different people wanting different things out of life.

"Oh well, I still have soccer," I thought. But then I learned that in order to walk on to play for the college soccer team, I needed to be a resident of Wisconsin for a full year, and I'd only been a resident for 11 months.

I was pretty bummed at the time. None of the reasons I had moved had come to fruition. My plan was blown to bits.

At first, I looked at this experience as a bust and a waste of time and money spent traveling halfway across the country. Even if I didn't know it then, that time became exactly what I needed. I had a great group of friends. I worked a 9-5 job, which taught me that office life was never going to be in the cards for me. I was given the freedom to come and go as I pleased and I had real genuine conversations with my elders who gave me incredible and invaluable life advice. Those things were not what I expected to get from this experience, but being there really allowed me to grow in ways I never expected. I didn't realize it at the time because life was happening quickly and I just moved on to the next thing. Before long, I started attending college back in Indiana.

That's life. It comes at us fast and from all angles. We often hear life compared to a roller coaster with all of the ups and downs. On a roller coaster, the drops are our favorite part. Yet in life, we don't like the drops. What if we started looking at the dips in life as the thrill of the ride?

Since our earliest stages of life, we have learned by our observations. Maybe we witnessed the stress that our parents endured from the vantage point of our carseats. Maybe something went "wrong" like the car suddenly got a flat, and instead of looking at it as a happenstance of life, the stress builds and our parents bicker about something that is out of their control. And that response becomes engrained in our minds as we observe their reactions. We conclude that's how you deal with things and get the false notion that somehow we should be able to control every situation. But we didn't, so now we're the unlucky souls of this godforsaken world.

When you start asking, "Why is this happening to me? What did I do to deserve this?" The simple truth is... You. Were. Born. That's what happened to you. Life wants to see how you are going to react.

I'll be honest, I used to react poorly to these kinds of situations. In my senior year of high school I worked part-time at an insurance company in a school-to-work program. I saved up my money to go visit a foreign exchange student my family had hosted (whom I consider a brother). When my mom and I set off on the journey to visit him in Turkey, the trip started off as a disaster. We missed our connecting flight in Atlanta and, when we finally arrived, our luggage didn't. I didn't have my clothes, my toothbrush, and most importantly a suit that I needed for a Turkish wedding we were planning to attend. I was pissed.

"What am I going to do? I have nothing! This fucking airline sucks!" But my mom and my brother from Turkey put things into perspective, reminding me that I was fine, I was in Turkey, and it wasn't like I would need a lot of clothes since we would be spending most of our time at the beach. My brother's dad took us to the tailor and I got a brand new suit made in Turkey! How many people get to say that? I was lucky enough to be where I was and surrounded by people I love. I could still have an amazing time, but I had let go of the lost luggage. (We ended up getting our lost luggage with 3 days left before we returned home from a 3-week trip.)

When we realize how many situations are out of our control, we can learn to let loose, we can observe the situation through a different perspective. We can use situations like lost luggage and flat tires to test ourselves. Maybe next time we have a new mindset. Maybe it has been a long time since we've changed a tire and this scenario will help us see if we've still got it! Or who knows, maybe some nice pedestrian will even stop and help out. We might even get to talking and find out that they work in the same field and there's an opening at their company. Thanks to a flat tire, you've suddenly got a great opportunity, or at least a new friend, or skill.

Bottom line is: you never know what life is going to throw at you. But when something does throw off your plan, remember that's it only your perspective that makes an experience negative or positive.

The opportunity to shine when you are confronted with an obstacle is, and always has been, how our species evolves.

Marcus Aurelius said it best: "The impediment to action advances action. What stands in the way becomes the way."

We evolve because of difficulties. If there were never challenges, we might still be finger-painting in caves with no idea what a selfie is. (Come to think of it, maybe let's slow down with the evolving.) But seriously, look back and consider the moments that changed you. What happened to you after a difficult period? Did you adjust your focus and learn from those difficulties? I'm guessing that when you persevered in the face of adversity, you experienced some type of breakthrough. When we acquire valuable lessons, we can apply those insights to situations that we face which helps us to perceive the world through a different lens – a world that is always aligned with our interests, even when it's not so obvious.

# TIPS:

Look at your life. Write about a time when you really struggled. How did you get out of the struggle? Or *did* you get out of that particular struggle? Looking back at it now, what would you do differently? What did you learn? What might have been the purpose of that experience compared with your expectations of the outcome?

Start observing your natural reactions and thoughts when you face difficult situations. Notice your patterns. Become aware of them, attempt to replace negative reactions with thoughts and actions that make way for growth.

**Resources:**

*The Obstacle is the Way,* by Ryan Holiday

*Meditations,* by Marcus Aurelius

# 6.
# Never Be The Victim

*"Self-pity is our worst enemy and if we yield to it, we can never do anything good in the world."*

**- Helen Keller**

Building on the previous chapter, thinking like a victim is about our perception. What we will discuss in this chapter is not just our attitude about life's obstacles, but also the ego that often overtakes our beliefs about the world and where we fit into it.

Before we dive in, there is something that must be addressed about the word "victim" here. There are definitely situations such as abuse, assault, murder, etc., when people are clearly victimized, and I am in no way disputing that reality. What I am referring to in this chapter is the lens we use to define ourselves. Even for individuals who have been a victim at some point in their lives, this chapter is about not letting "victim" become one's identity.

Since birth, I have always been a hyper-sensitive person. My parents would tell you that I went from joyful laughter to utter fury in a matter of seconds, even as a toddler. I'd like to say this tendency ended during childhood, but this is a non-fiction book. So I must admit that my emotional sensitivity carried over well into my adult years. I'd let everything affect me.

If I experienced a low, I'd jump to the conclusion that the outside world was always out to get me. When I was riding an emotional high, I wondered when the world would turn on me and destroy the happiness I was experiencing. If life was good, I deserved it. And if it felt bad, I was the victim who would think to myself, "I'm a good person, why is this unfortunate thing happening to me?"

When I figured out that life isn't singling me out and that there isn't some invisible arm trying to hold me down, I realized I'm not a victim. I'm not an unlucky character in a story. I'm just like everyone else. And everyone experiences the ebbs and flows of this thing called life.

Why was I always thinking of myself as a victim? How did I crawl out of the hole of despair and self-victimization? I was only able to stop being a victim when I learned that I had the ability to make simple adjustments to end my self-tormenting pattern.

Changing this habit started with a simple question. Every time I started to respond like a victim I would ask myself, "Why?" Not, "Why is this happening to me?" But rather, "Why am I responding as if I have no control?"

I *do* have control. But not in the way I first wanted. I can't control outside circumstances, but I do have control over how I react to a perceived slight. For example, I misread my departure time for my flight and got stuck at the airport for the next 15 hours. (Yes, this happened to me.) I can react by asking questions to reframe the situation. *What can I learn from this? How can I spend my time at the airport in a productive and helpful way to grow? Do I sit at the bar and drink the time away, or do I pull out my journal and write down my thoughts about this moment and the amazing trip I just completed? Do I take this inconvenient moment personally and be the victim or do I shrug it off and become the victor of the moment?*

We all have choices to make when facing every obstacle that comes along. If you come to the realization that you're playing the victim and that you have a choice, think about why you started playing this role in the first place. What's it doing for you?

For me, it came down to the realization that I wanted to *love* and *be loved* so badly that whenever things didn't go my way, I took it personally. In short, I was not being unconditional with my love and acceptance of others or of life. I expected the universe, along with the people in it, to always reward me - to "love me back" in a sense - for being a good person. It was a horrible way of living, always setting myself up for disappointment and relying on the outside world to fulfill me.

I would learn that, when constantly trying to get my validation from others, the appreciation I received never lived up to my expectations. In turn, I was always a victim.

No one and no thing can make us feel whole. Another pat on the back isn't going to make us feel as good as the reward of love we feel inside ourselves for being true to ourselves, doing the right thing, and knowing we are making a positive impact on the world around us. Other people can't read our minds or know exactly what we need, nor is it anyone else's responsibility to give us what we need.

Another common occasion for painting ourselves as victims is during disagreements. We take our own side from our viewpoint because we can see it clearly. But our vantage point doesn't have to be all that fits on our screen. How we deal with challenges and disputes determines our character and our outlook on life. Yet so many things in the world today are painted as black and white. Us versus them, or good guys versus the evil empire. But, in reality, most issues, disputes, rights, and wrongs fall into grey areas. Almost always, no one is entirely right in any given disagreement.

Let's say you and your partner have an argument. You've been busy at work and working overtime to afford the engagement ring of your partner's dreams. But, not only have you got a long way to go before you've saved enough money for the ring, you just got passed over for a promotion that was given to someone you think isn't deserving. Your frustration leads you to distance yourself from your partner who has been agitated with you for being too preoccupied with work.

So they start giving you the cold shoulder and things begin going downhill in your relationship. You're pissed. You have been working so hard and sacrificing your free time to please your partner and surprise them with the perfect engagement ring. Your partner is pissed because they have no idea what's going on with you, so their mind is wandering aimlessly with thoughts of abandonment and deception. How you both react to this scenario has a huge impact on your relationship and its survival.

In times like these, we naturally go to our friends and get advice. So let's say you decide to let off some steam and you head to your local watering hole for an ice-cold beverage of your choice. You have a seat, order your drink, and like most local bars, there are some familiar regulars here. You exchange small talk and they can tell you're down. When they ask you what's up, you tell them you're having a problem with your partner, who has confronted you about being more attentive and asked to take a break to reevaluate the relationship.

The folks at the bar immediately come to your defense. "How dare your partner say you aren't attentive? You've been there for them, and look what you're trying to do to make sure they get their dream engagement ring!" "They are lucky you're their partner!" The whole bar of acquaintances supports you while they bash your partner.

Your beliefs have been validated, so now you're feeling good. You want some fresh air to bask in your glory, so you head to the patio of the bar and take a sip of your tasty beverage with a big smile on your face. The folks out here notice how happy you seem. When they ask you what's up, you tell them of your "former" relationship problem. To your surprise, the folks out on the patio aren't nodding their heads in agreement. These folks have questions:

"Have there been any recent changes in your schedule?"

"Did anything happen at work that has impacted your time together?"

"How did you react to what they said?"

"How do you think you should respond?"

While answering their questions, you realize maybe you weren't completely in the right after all.

The difference between these two groups' responses matters. The first group places all of the blame on your partner. They support you by putting the other person down without questioning your perspective in the dispute. They've got your back 100 percent.

The second group supports you by asking questions so you can make the best decision possible. They know it takes two to fight and that most conflicts arise because of unclear communication. They have your back 100% too, just in a different way. Both offer support, but one example places you as the victim. The other represents a wide picture view of the situation. You are trying to do something nice and you expect your partner to know that. Your partner gives you the cold shoulder when they notice a change in your behavior. Neither of you have been communicating. This isn't their fault, it isn't your fault, you <u>both</u> have responsibility in this lack of communication.

The group at the bar are not real friends. They are only telling you what you want to hear. They are living the victim lifestyle. Nothing they (or you) do could ever possibly be wrong, in their opinion.

You need to move over to the patio table where true friends are not only supporting you, they are also telling you where you fucked up. They realize that no one is perfect, that we make mistakes, and that you are only a victim if you choose to be a victim.

By changing your outlook, and possibly your friend group, you are making the choice to expand your perception and your responses to life. By looking at every occurrence from a bird's eye view, you are seeing what you have done wrong and how others could have perceived your gestures or comments as a slight.

When you stop acting and thinking like a victim, you can evaluate without criticizing. You can begin communicating with yourself and others in a neutral way. This isn't easy at first, but no great achievement is ever accomplished overnight. It takes time and practice. The first step in correcting the victim mentality is to realize that we are usually part of the problem, either by our actions or our reactions.

## TIPS:

This shift cannot occur until you begin doing good unconditionally, just because it makes you feel good and you know it's right, rather than expecting anyone to reward you. So practice! The next time you're in line at the grocery store or grabbing a bite to eat, pay for the person behind you or tip the cashier really well, then move along quickly. Don't wait around long enough for a thank you. Do this simply because you want to, with no other reason and see how good it feels.

Whenever the next disagreement or conflict occurs with someone in your life, look at your actions first rather than the other person's. What part did you play in this disagreement? What would you like say to yourself if you were the other person? After taking the opportunity to look at the ways your actions or reactions contributed to the situation, how would you respond differently if you could go back and do it again? Try that approach the next time you engage in a conflict or misunderstanding.

# PART II:
# Learn

# 7.
# Speak Your Truth

———◆———

*"In the long run the most unpleasant truth is a safer companion than a pleasant falsehood."*

**- Theodor Roosevelt**

"Be polite." "Don't say anything you'll regret."

"If you don't have something nice to say, don't say anything at all."

These are the lessons we have been taught since we were children. Basically, don't offend anyone or step on their toes. But, to be honest, this is bullshit. Yes, you can and should be kind, but no matter how hard you try to never hurt anyone's feelings, it is going to happen. You *will* say things you regret. And, more often than not, the things you *don't* say will hurt others, too.

If it seems that people get offended by the smallest things, remember that it's often their past experiences, fears, or unhealed trauma that cause them to react to you. But their reaction doesn't mean you don't speak your truth. Since you can't control how anyone will react to your words, what's the point of suppressing your true feelings or holding back what you need to say? What good can come from being dishonest or saying nothing at all to avoid someone's reaction?

There are a couple of common ways most of us tend to be dishonest in relationships. The first is failing to address legitimate issues in order to avoid conflict. For example, if you decide to not consult your boss about your displeasure with a project or how a co-worker's behavior has negatively affected you, in short, your true feelings keep boiling up inside and have no way to be released. And when there is nowhere for them to go, get ready for an implosion or an explosion. Letting anger or bitterness fester will only lead to resentment. And resentment isn't on anyone but ourselves. Yes, it seems easier to blame someone else than, god forbid, accepting responsibility for our own actions. Getting uncomfortable and expressing our true thoughts and emotions leads to stronger, more honest relationships with others and even with ourselves.

A second way dishonesty enters into many relationships is when we change our words or behaviors to appease someone. We just tell them what they want to hear or make ourselves into what we think they want us to be. But when we change ourselves for someone else, we are not being true to ourselves. And, whether we realize it or not, it's obvious. Even if it isn't immediately evident to the casual observer, it doesn't take long for someone to detect that something feels off.

We have probably all cringed around people who show off to impress others by exaggerating how important, or successful, or interesting they are. We can tell when an egomaniac is over-compensating for a lack of confidence. Something in our gut tells us we can't fully trust this person.

This doesn't just happen with strangers or friends. It's just as common in romantic relationships, when partners try to conform to fit what the other person wants or what we *think* they want. I used to change myself for other people all the time. I would think my partner and I needed to have a lot in common and enjoy doing the same activities, even if I didn't truly enjoy those things. So, I would go along and pretend to enjoy the things they enjoyed.

In time, this shapeshifting behavior becomes obvious and it's actually much more risky to pretend than to simply be your-self. No one is *that* good of an actor.

But let's say you succeed and this person "likes" you, but in reality, they don't actually know you. They like the fictional version of you that you have created. That's an exhausting facade to put on. Eventually, you will show your true colors, otherwise you live the rest of your life as a miserable shell of a person who is not fully living.

Being true to who you are - to your core character - allows you to navigate your goals, aspirations, and gifts in order to be your true self. Living and speaking your truth helps free you to be your true self and allow yourself to be known by the people you want in your life.

Just as habitual liars are formed by repetition, so is speak-ing your truth. Rather than avoiding honest conversations and changing yourself for other people, let yourself be known. In reality, you probably have no idea what anyone wants you to be. They may not even know what they want to be themselves.

When I first moved out to Los Angeles I met an acting coach and all-around amazing person named Steve Braun. Steve is the co-founder of BGB Studios, a very successful acting studio, and he has had such an impact on countless individuals who have walked through his acting studio doors.

The method Steve teaches is about acting your truth. It's not about pulling ideas out of thin air, but being true to how you are and how you feel in each and every given moment. Emotions change by the second, so he taught us to recognize each emotion, then express that emotion. The more clearly we communicate our feelings, the less distortion and miscommunication will happen.

Steve uses the Meisner repetition exercise in his classes, where two people stare at each other and one says exactly how they feel in that moment and the other person must repeat it so they can truly take it in:

"I like you."

"You like me."

"I want to punch your face."

"You want to punch my face."

This exchange helps both people connect, stay true to their feelings in the moment and to express them, rather than containing them out of fear of hurting the other person's feelings. And it assures both people that they are being heard because they must repeat it back.

What is *not* allowed in this exercise is name calling or any physical altercation. Believe me, they do happen from time to time. The reason for no physical interactions is obvious, of course violence is not tolerated. But banning name-calling is just as important because it keeps people from putting labels on each other. And the truth is, we are all nice sometimes and assholes on occasion.

Name-calling is also a form of avoidance of real feelings, and can even be an attempt to stir up a response from someone else rather than letting them have a natural response of their own. If I call you a "fucking rat bastard" what I really mean is I don't like you. Name-calling is a cop-out that keeps us from expressing an actual feeling, such as, "I feel intimidated around you".

It's interesting doing this exercise when someone is holding onto something that has been unexpressed and they're trying to avoid feeling it. After observing and participating in this exercise, I am convinced that living according to the Meisner repetition exercise would help us all resolve conflicts far more quickly, with strangers and loved ones alike. Wars could have even been prevented, along with disagreements about land and ownership of property, if only people had been able to say what they really want and need, and had the freedom honestly express how they felt.

All we have to offer each other in this life are bits of ourselves. People we have one-time encounters with can be changed by what we say and how we interact with them, not to mention the people we interact with frequently. What a tragedy it is to hold back from speaking our truth for any reason, especially if fear and discomfort are keeping us from connecting with the people in our lives. Take the leap of faith and speak your truth, because that is what the world deserves, and it's what *you* deserve.

## **TIPS:**

Write down the times you wish you had spoken up and said something more honest about how you felt. What do you wish you had said differently? Now say those things, whether out loud or in your mind.

Do you feel better? Does it feel more natural than holding it in?

I urge you to take this practice out into the real world. If you catch yourself not being truthful, correct your course the moment you become aware that you're holding back. Speak your truth. The more often you do this, the more quickly you will create a positive habit that will profoundly impact you and everyone around you.

Yes, remember to be polite. But always be honest. Rather than reacting, a few great segues to politely express your truth are:

"That sounds interesting, and I think..."

"I understand that is how you feel and I respect that. This is the way I feel..."

"I know this may just be my point of view, and I feel like I would regret not saying this..."

# 8.
# Enjoy Being Wrong



*"It is better to change an opinion than to persist in a wrong one."*

**- Socrates**

Stop thinking that you are right, stop wanting to always be right, and start to enjoy, yes I said *enjoy* being wrong. Being wrong is so damn unpopular, but in our adult lives, one of the only ways we ever learn anything new is to realize we are wrong. And that makes being wrong exciting!

It's easy to get so caught up in winning an argument that we don't care if we are actually right or not. We just want to <u>win</u> that argument, so we get louder for the sole purpose of drowning out anyone who disagrees with us. We "put them in their place" and stomp any contradiction they have to our opinion, even if we have no idea what we're talking about!

We do this, not because we are experts on the topic at hand, but because we feel so strongly about our opinion that we can't imagine that it could possibly be wrong. And, if we start identifying ourselves with the answers we are so determined to protect, no matter how inaccurate they may be, being challenged feels personal. Being wrong isn't a slight against us. But as long as we approach conversations in this way, we will never come to accept other viewpoints. If we are going to evolve into wiser versions of ourselves, this part of our ego that gets attached to certain ideas and beliefs needs to go.

In Adam Grant's book, *Think Again: The Power of Knowing What You Don't Know*, he talks about the significance of "thinking like a "scientist" and its importance of testing everything before we determine what we believe. But not just testing once, but again and again at all times because what was true or knowable yesterday may be proven differently today or tomorrow. That's why science continually makes new breakthroughs. That's why there are always new revelations about concepts that we once believed were true and now find out that it may not be so. For example, green dye used to be made from arsenic. And we used to handle mercury without a second thought. Heroin was used as cough syrup in the past! All of these discoveries were big breakthroughs in their day. But, after more research and learning throughout the years, better, safer solutions replaced what we now know were dangerous practices.

The scientific mindset questions what we think we know by conducting experiments and following the evidence then continuing to test that evidence. From there, we develop a theory. This stage of discovery isn't called a fact because at some point any theory can be upended by some new discovery!

Nothing is ever 100 percent sure. Things we used to swear were true always become clearer with time, as we learn more. The ability to rethink our approach to pretty much anything will take us to places we would never find by digging in our heels with wrong or outdated information. When we become less concerned about being right and more concerned about learning, then we begin to evolve and acquire more and more knowledge. Remaining open-minded and nurturing our child-like curiosity leads to continuous learning, which actually helps us enjoy being wrong. When we can accept being wrong with open arms, we are able to defeat the ego and free ourselves to enter every conversation and discussion without defensiveness, as if we know nothing.

Be aware, however, that the ego will never be eradicated entirely. It's always lingering in the background, waiting for opportunities to reappear. It may show up as a persistent thought or a bodily sensation that is trying to pull us into reactivity. Our ego has been with us throughout our lives and knows us so well. Since adolescence, our egos have been building a false sense of knowledge and accompanying illusion that we know what is actually going on in the world. We rebel against our parents because they don't understand us. And when we are given certain liberties as adults, many of us even rebel against society, thinking those liberties mean we have arrived at adulthood and are all done growing. We think we know what life is all about even when we allow our freedoms to cloud our judgement about what we *do* and *don't* know. We aren't all-powerful, all-knowing beings. We are discoverers, explorers; we are scientists. Just think, humans discovered how to make fire 1.5 million years ago and today we are still learning new ways to contain them and put them out.

Let's just embrace the fact that we don't know everything, then we can look ahead with excitement about what we might learn every single day and in every conversation we have. Let's rediscover the days when we learned to raise our hand in class and ask questions or make a guess at the answers. Let's take the risk of being wrong. And let's not just be *willing* to be wrong, but *embrace* it. Invite it, even!

When we become more aware of our blind spots as individuals, we discover that *who we are* and *what we know* can change in really important ways. Even our taste buds change over time, so why not accept that our attitudes about life might need to change, too?

## **TIPS:**

Type into Google: "false facts that people think are true" and cross reference those false facts with five credible sources to back them up. After you do that, you still can't trust that what you read was 100% true. Investigate more.

Type into Google: "things we used to think were safe and discovered they weren't."

The next time you are in a conversation and realize you're wrong, take a breath. If you start to feel that old anger boil up, it's okay to tell someone, "I need a second." Then, step away for fresh air or a moment of solitude to gather yourself. Ask why you are getting so upset and sit with that. Look at the conversation from the other person's perspective. What would you have said or done if you were them reacting to your words? Answer this honestly for yourself.

Try to feel how you would feel in their place. You may feel differently than how they feel, but this is an important way to imagine yourself on the other side of the discussion.

When you're ready to go back to the discussion, let them know your emotions got the best of you and that you're working on it. If you screwed up and overreacted at first, acknowledge that and let them know you appreciate them teaching you a different perspective. We are all works in progress and most people in your life will appreciate your honesty and vulnerability.

Next time you have a conversation with someone who tells you something you don't believe is true, express curiosity and ask more about their viewpoint. Observe whether or not they know more than you about the subject. If they don't, rather than correcting them in the moment or telling them they are wrong, note their points and do more research on it the next chance you get. You'll be amazed what you can learn with this approach. The internet is a powerful resource, but be careful not to always refer to the same websites that validate your viewpoint. You might even look up experts in a particular field and send them an e-mail to ask for their input. But, no matter what, keep in mind that no one will ever know everything. Nothing is 100% true.

**Resources:**

*Think Again: The Power of Knowing What You Don't Know,* by Adam Grant

# 9.
# We Get By With a Little Help From Our (True) Friends

*"I long to see you so that I may impart to you some spiritual gift to make you strong — that is, that you and I may be mutually encouraged by each other's faith."*

**- Romans 1:11-12 NIV**

What's so scary about going down this path of change? For me, it was facing my demons head on. But doing that alone would have been even more terrifying.

Tackling challenges that have been haunting us for years is going to be frustrating at times. There are times when it's natural to question whether or not progress is even possible. But if you are tempted to think no one will ever understand what you're going through, take it from me. That's not the case. Maybe your friends don't know exactly how you feel, but there are many people who are on a similar path, or who have been in the past, and can relate. It's essential to find these people and surround yourself with them. Whether it's true friends, a therapist, a mentor who can help guide you along the path of self-improvement, or all of the above, you will be amazed how others can and will help you along the way.

Unlike some self-improvement enthusiasts, I do not agree with the notion that therapy isn't for everyone. I believe therapy is truly necessary. Just as with finding the right friends and mentors, the right therapist will need to be a good fit with your worldview and personality.

A good therapist helps you learn how to rediscover yourself and understand the feelings behind your actions. It's a chance to dive in and see what makes you *you*. But even the greatest therapists can't do the work for you. The amount of effort and vulnerability you bring to the process makes all the difference.

Are some people capable of doing this without therapy? Maybe. But those individuals are few and far between, in my opinion. And those folks most likely have a strong support system around them or a mentor who is guiding them along. If you are currently taking this journey without a therapist, I urge you to consider the extra benefits of therapy.

Even if we think we know ourselves well, it's easy to overlook our own faults. Whether we choose to ignore them to make ourselves feel better or we are genuinely unaware, the version of ourselves that *we* know can be quite different from the version of us that *others* know.

Sociologist Charles Horton Cooley wrote, "I am not what I think I am, and I am not what you I think I am. I am what I think you think I am." So often we lose ourselves trying to be what we think others want us to be. But living like this can slowly diminish our true character. If we have a good support system around us and true friends, we will have allies in our growth and will not feel the need to morph our personalities to impress them. As we learn how to disarm ourselves without fear of rejection, our support people are able to help us know when we step out of line and aren't being our best selves. This is why surrounding ourselves with safe, trustworthy folks is so essential.

Typically, we allow outside influences to change who we are for one of two reasons. The first is a positive one-- we want to grow, and true friends encourage us and point out our flaws to keep us in check. True friends will help us see where we have room for improvement if we are open to their input. True friends help us change for internal reasons. We listen to what they think because we care about them and respect their opinions, knowing they want what is best for us. Generally, our friends and family will be as truthful with us as we are with them. Together, we build each other up and grow simultaneously, especially if we have a shared interest in facing ourselves and breaking through our barriers.

The second reason is one we almost all get sucked into at some point. We can change in not-so-great ways because we worry about what people think of us. This fear causes us to change for external reasons, because we don't want to be rejected. We long for acceptance, so we want to wow a love interest. We want to impress co-workers who go to all of the cool spots for happy hour. We we want to fit in and we worry we aren't good enough, we change who we are. Falling into this habit causes us to start hiding who we truly are or we start becoming who we think others want us to be. This is a slippery slope. The more you do this, the harder it is to find yourself through all of the layers of bullshit you have been piling on.

I mentioned early on that I was a smoker for fifteen years. The first cigarette I had was when I was on spring break in high school. All of my friends were smoking in a hotel room, because now we were done with athletics, we were done with high school, we were now "men." Not to mention all of the girls we were meeting were smoking cigarettes, too. Up to this point I had always loathed cigarettes and vowed I'd never smoke one. Well, I wanted to fit in, I wanted to be cool. I didn't want my friends or these new potential love interests to think I was lame. I always knew it was a terrible habit to pick up, but I never thought I would become reliant on smoking, nor did I imagine I'd want to use it as a tool to harm myself. I fell down the slippery slope.

Doing things to fit in can also create pathological liars. Pathological liars don't become that way overnight. They begin with a little lie. Then that little lie turns into a bigger lie and before you know it they rely on nothing but lies because that is all they know. Stop lying to yourself and stop worrying about how others perceive you.

As a whole, we care way too much about what other people think, and often these people are perfect strangers or just acquaintances.

I used to attend many networking events with powerful and "important" people in Hollywood. These are the people I thought I needed to have in my life and in my corner in order to be successful. I would never let my guard down and be myself because I was constantly worrying, "Did I say something wrong?" "What will they think of me?" "Don't say anything stupid!" I thought I needed their approval and that they were really analyzing my every word and action. But I would discover, in truth, most people are too busy worrying about their own issues to care about anyone else's.

According to author Mark Manson, in *The Subtle Art of Not Giving a F*ck,* we would all be better off if we did what the title says and stop giving a fuck about situations and people that don't matter! The way to learn more about yourself is through good honest relationships with people who will challenge you and question you on your bullshit, but they know who you are and love every part of you.

Having a therapist is important in addition to relying on your true friends because, for starters, it's not your true friends' jobs to just help you improve. It is a therapist's job though. They study behavior for a living. They are unbiased and most likely don't know you on a friendship level. You can practice speaking your truth without the fear of being judged. Your whole interaction with them can be the actual word vomit that fills your mind on a daily basis.

Good therapists, like your true friends, want you to become the best version of you that you can be. But, unlike friendships, this entire relationship is focused on you and all the energy in the room is about you. Having all that energy on you can be intimidating at times, because then you see faults that you have been hiding or denying for years, you are forced to tackle all that baggage. You are faced with the trauma that has shaped you. It's scary, but it's also the best environment for discovering yourself, especially any traumas that need to be addressed.

Of the countless people we meet throughout our lives, those we let in, and the way we let them influence us, makes all the difference. Not allowing anyone in is not an option, so choose carefully. And, even though some people can do this journey of growth on their own, it would be like hiking Everest without a sherpa: You might eventually get there, but the journey will be longer and much more difficult and you better be traveling with a group. No one, and I mean *no one* can do this alone. You must have support, because there is no solo climb to the summit.

## TIPS:

Think about your current friend group and see who is actually truthful with you. What activities do you and your friends do together? What do you talk about? Whose opinions do you trust? Who comes to you with their serious life problems? Who do you go to? If you don't have anyone you can confide in, maybe it's time to get some new friends.

If a friend isn't being real with you, holding you accountable for your actions, or being a positive influence, maybe that person isn't someone you actually need in your life. Walking away from relationships can be incredibly difficult to do, but often necessary.

I had a friend who is one of the best people in the world and he was my closest friend for nearly a decade. He was always so kind and helpful, but I wasn't an equally good friend to him. He continued to be that good friend, even during our departure, by telling me that he didn't feel the friendship was balanced enough and I was unaware when he was in need. At the time, his honesty hurt me tremendously. But now, I credit him for allowing me to spread my wings and fly. After he shared his perspective with me, I was able to reflect and see where I had screwed up and where I needed to make changes. I miss this friend dearly, but I wouldn't be the person I am or where I am in life, without his honest approach. He explained where things went wrong and how I affected him. He was honest and upfront with how he felt. Rather than ghosting me or making up excuses, he laid out the facts.

There will probably be times when friendships need to change or end if your friends are just not on the same path as you. No matter your circumstances when a friendship needs to end, be honest. Telling the truth will allow your friend to reflect and face some of their own demons. Just don't be a dick.

If you're looking to meet new people who might become the true friends you need, try Meetup app, or become more involved in hobbies or volunteer opportunities that interest you. There are probably a lot of good people who share your interests who are looking for a friend, too.

I'm not going to give you medical advice, since I am not a medical expert, but I highly encourage you to seek out therapists who are available in your area. Many organizations offer free mental health services or try using a low-cost app like BetterHelp so you have the support you need to heal and evolve.

**Resources:**

www.betterhelp.com

The Subtle Art of Not Giving a F*ck, by Mark Manson

Meetup App

# 10.
# Learn From Those Who Came Before You

*"Wisdom belongs to the aged, and understanding to the old."*

**- Job 12:12 NLT**

*Please note: Throughout this chapter, I will use the word parents as a general term for the people that had the largest impact in raising you.

We don't get to choose our parents. Some of us got lucky and some of us got screwed over. But we can all say, no matter how great or terrible our upbringing was, parents have a huge impact on the people we become, for better or worse. Whether we got the cream of the crop, the bottom of the barrel, or somewhere in-between, parents are the people we learn from first and foremost.

They are the ones we mimicked when we were younger. They are the ones who taught us their versions of right and wrong. They are the ones we leaned on and looked to for guidance during troubled times. And we probably have all witnessed times when circumstances got the best of them, and we learned from them in those times, too.

Eleanor Roosevelt said that we need to "learn from the mistakes of others. You can't live long enough to make them all yourself." Who better to learn from than the people who have had the most influence on our life from the start?

Whether your parents were the ideal role models or the definition of "People Who Should Not Procreate," you can learn so much from them. Examining the trials and tribulations they encountered helps you learn from their failures and successes. You can learn just as much, if not more, from people who have failed than from those who have succeeded, whether by observation or asking questions. But so often, we forget to take advantage of this opportunity with our parents.

We live in a society where we are told we aren't supposed to be friends with our parents until an older age, if ever. But I say that's garbage. We are wasting one of our most valuable resources in life if we are afraid to ask our parents tough questions. Find out what it took for them to succeed, ask about their failures, and find out what they regret the most in life and why.

Listening to your parents' answers to your questions can help you discover more about *them* and *yourself*. You'll discover things that you may not consider all that important now, but they will take on new meaning later in life. These conversations allow you to see life from a different perspective and through the eyes of people who have been playing the game a lot longer than you.

The goal is not to take their experiences and make them your beliefs. It's important to be true to yourself and be willing to take risks, go against advice, and experience life through your own eyes. But rather hold on to the knowledge you learn from your parents and keep it in the back of your mind to apply, if necessary, to your own circumstances. You've still got to write your own story, but life notes from the people who raised you may inspire your journey and take you to new places you may not discover otherwise.

In Chapter 5, I told you how my dad is a very logical person. Well, when I was about 8 or 9 years old my dad did something that was out of character, and something that I'm sure made him uncomfortable. He quit his job because he was unhappy. He knew this was a risk, but he also believed in himself enough to bet on himself. He attempted and failed at a few business ventures he started on his own. But then he was able to successfully start his own consulting business. This business has given him the freedom to work for himself, to do things his way. He showed me that, if you really believe in yourself, you can do anything. I know I wouldn't have had the guts to move to LA without witnessing his well-placed bet. He probably has no idea how much this affected me.

You don't have to stop with your parents. When I moved cross country I drove with my grandpa - "Gramps" as I called him. He was one of my best friends until the day he died. I learned so much from this man and I am so lucky to have spent such valuable one-on-one time with him. We did two cross country road trips and spent several week-long vacations together. What he taught me was how to live a life of balance. You can work hard, but also play hard. Our road trips provided quality time we got to spend together, while also checking places off his bucket list. We went to Mt. Rushmore, The Grand Canyon, Bryce Canyon, Yellowstone, Glacier National Park... hell, we even went hang-gliding on one family trip. He truly taught me that life is short and it's up to us to make the most of it.

Almost all of our elders would love to offer guidance through their stories as long as we're receptive. Decades ago, it seems society had so much more respect for their elders and would lean on older generations for life advice.

Native Americans didn't write down their knowledge. They relied on verbal communication and vivid narratives to pass on their history, rituals, and legends. If the elders spoke, the younger generations would listen and ask questions. Unfortunately, as a whole, both the elders and younger generations today do not have the kind of mutual respect that fosters healthy conversation. Somewhere along the way, we've stopped listening and don't try very hard to understand one another.

So many young people think their lives are so different than when their elders grew up. They think their elders are out of touch. They think their elders really don't care about a young person's future. Some write elders off as cranky old people.

On the other hand, elders often think the younger generation is lazy. We hear comments about how technological advances have made life too comfortable for the younger generation. Or how rude and ungrateful youngsters are. Some even write off younger generations as spoiled brats.

These conflicting perspectives have kept generations at odds with one another for years, and neither perspective is wrong. Our lives have changed at a rapid pace thanks to technology, but some elders forget that they, too, benefit from technology. They were once young and naive and treated as *less than* by their elders. They were once doing some of the same shenanigans they scold the younger generations for doing now.

There was a time when transportation across the Atlantic was new and affordable, and not just for the elite. The world shrank for some people, who could go back and forth and see more of the world. Yet this very change also created challenges for those who could see what amazing opportunities exist but never be within their grasp. Does this example sound like a similar dilemma younger people face now with social media? Seeing how glamorous life could be? When technology surpasses our basic needs, we tend to lust for more and more. And that longing can create lack of gratitude for what we currently have. All generations experience this with every advancement in the outside world. The true advancements, however, start from inside us and they don't leave us clamoring for more and more. They don't have the ironic effects of being *more* connected and *less* connected all at once.

We're still challenged by many of the same struggles that made life difficult centuries ago. We will always have the basic human needs of food, water, shelter, companionship. These are essential to our existence. We will still feel sadness, anger, and betrayal. We still love and experience loss. We all know what it's like to feel lost in the world without a sense of direction. Yes, the world constantly changes, but the basic challenges humans face also remains constant.

Remember that everyone who is young now will someday become the elders of the next generation. So, let's take the time to reach out to those who have been experiencing life for fifty, sixty, seventy years. They have made it this far and presumably nearer to the finish line. Why not seek out their advice, find out what paths they took, and maybe learn which ones they overlooked and wished they hadn't? I would advise that when you're young, have friends who are older than you, for the older can provide you with knowledge. And when you're older have friends who are younger than you, for they can provide you with energy and can challenge your ways.

When we take time with our parents and elders, we get tips for life. We get a jumpstart. And we don't have to stop with people we know. Books are a great way to learn from those who came before us. We can learn from people who are literally saints, and people who conquered the world, and even those who used their powers for evil. All of these people have something to teach us if we choose to be receptive.

As we gather this insight, we can either use it or ignore it. We all have "told you so" moments when we have been warned, but we ignore the warning signs. That's okay. We need to experience things for ourselves, but knowing what other people did in similar circumstances never hurts. Being open to learning from others doesn't mean we have to hold onto that information like it's the gospel. We can remain receptive, while also knowing that something that has worked for someone else may not work for us. But having others' knowledge and experiences in our back pocket might just come in handy later down the line.

# TIPS:

Ask your parents questions about some of the tough problems that you are currently facing. Find out what they did to persevere in similar situations. Find out what some of their biggest regrets are in life. What would they do differently looking back at it all?

Visit a retirement home or connect with older people in your community and befriend some elders who are not related to you. Make time regularly, maybe once every month or so, to get to know them better. Learn their story. Find out what they did in life and how they look at their life in retrospect. Not only will you gain a wealth of knowledge, you may bring a flood of energy to your elders.

**Resources:**

Song: "Everybody's Free to Wear Sunscreen" by Baz Luhrmann

# 11.
# Beliefs and Your Character

❖

*"...Don't go by reports, by legends, by traditions, by scripture, by logical conjecture, by inference, by analogies, by agreement through pondering views, by probability, or by the thought, 'This contemplative is our teacher.' When you know for yourselves that, 'These qualities are skillful; these qualities are blameless; these qualities are praised by the wise; these qualities, when adopted & carried out, lead to welfare & to happiness' — then you should enter & remain in them."*

**- The Buddha**

Beliefs alone are a lazy way of living. Most of us are busy believing things rather than experiencing them. We are born into this world as pure beings, regardless of our location or circumstances. As we grow older, when we begin to imitate behavior for the responses they produce, that purity is diminished.

Naturally, our environments and upbringing have a huge impact on our early development, so the people we imitate, our beliefs, and our traumas stick with us well into our adult years, and in many cases, until our death.

I often tell my friends on this journey of self-growth that I feel like our discovery is about finding who we were before we decided to let the world and others' opinions have any influence over us. We are learning who we were before the world had its say. Essentially, we are growing to learn who we were when we were young and innocent.

When we are toddlers there are no stereotypes, no judgement of people, places, or things, whether based on their appearance or what we have heard from a third-party. On the playground, we play with anyone and everyone until one kid takes a toy right out of our hands. Then we may cry and pout, but usually we forgive the other person and go grab another toy as if nothing ever happened. But if that same kid takes the next toy out of our hands, we may lose trust in this kid. We may think twice about going near them on the playground again. This is the process of learning by our own experience.

In just a few short years, we will overhear and understand adults when they make comments about other people's appearance or how that guy is an asshole because he cut them off at that intersection. We start to pick up the attitudes and beliefs of our elders and role models, and we are shaped by our environment as a whole. And as this happens, we begin to think less for ourselves and more about how others will think about what we say and do.

I grew up in the Midwest, in Indianapolis, Indiana. I lived in the suburbs of the city, but I went to school thirty minutes away, in the middle of the farmland most people envision when they hear Indiana. I love my hometown and still have a lot of friends and family that live there. Back in 2008 there was a proposition to legalize same-sex marriage in California. I had a discussion with someone from back home about it. This person, John, was opposed to same-sex marriage. Where we grew up, homophobic slang was used commonly and LGBTQ+ rights were very limited. In the early 90s and 2000s not a lot of folks in Indiana were openly LGBTQ+ and meeting someone who was open was not a common occurrence. This is not an excuse for John's discrimination of the LGBTQ+ community, but he was opposed to same-sex marriage because he didn't know anyone who was LGBTQ+. Since he didn't have a direct connection, he didn't empathize with people in that community. John is a religious guy and we grew up in a time and place where being LGBTQ+ was looked at as sinful and marriage was sacred only between a man and a woman.

But John's perspective changed when he moved into a new neighborhood next door to a gay couple. When John and his wife met the couple next door, as with most introductions, their occupations came up in conversation. John had recently been let go from his job and his new neighbors told John of an opportunity at their workplace. They put in a call and John got an interview and he ended up getting the job. Over time, John's views began to change.

He was no longer relying on his old beliefs, which were highly influenced by the social environment he grew up in. His opinion had been crafted by other people's beliefs which were instilled in him. Similar to seeing an ad or hearing a review from someone else, his information was all secondhand until his encounter with his new neighbors changed his viewpoint.

We have all been John at some point in our lives. We have all carried a viewpoint that was based solely on our beliefs rather than our own experiences.

The fact is, there is no better teacher in life than our experiences. Getting out there and getting our hands dirty with real life experiences reveals who we really are at our core. We absolutely can and we should learn from others. But other people cannot be the only source of our perspectives. We need to reconfirm or discover for ourselves.

Beliefs are formed by sitting on the sidelines and never getting in the game. Beliefs that often go unquestioned, then get passed on through generations, lead to corruption. When we rely solely on beliefs, we don't live our lives to the fullest. It's like watching the trailer and thinking we know the whole plot to the movie.

Experience is not only *seeing* the movie, but getting to *be* in it. We are the lead characters in our lives and we deserve top billing. But, just like all lead characters, when we have our ups and downs, they are ours alone. We share them with no one else. Can we let others know about these experiences so they can support us? Absolutely. But our experiences themselves are unique to us. And with every experience, we peel off another layer of the onion of who we are when we choose not to give in to whatever others say or believe. By discovering *for* ourselves we *discover* ourselves.

# TIPS:

Write down some beliefs you have never tried, questioned, or experienced for yourself. (And I'm not saying to go out there and do every drug on the planet or try things that have been proven by science to be deadly.) But, for example, if vegan cheese sounds disgusting but you've never tried it... then try it. Start small, like a food that's not normally in your wheelhouse, then work your way up to bigger experiences like skydiving, taking public transportation, or chanting with monks on a Sunday morning. After you have experienced something new, go back to your journal and write down how it made you feel. Did you enjoy it? Did you hate it? Did it differ from what others have told you about their belief of it?

**Resources:**

*Think Again: The Power of Knowing What You Don't Know,* by Adam Grant

# PART III:
## Act

# 12.
# The Time to Be Present is Now

*"When you make the present moment, instead of the past and future the focal point of your life, your ability to enjoy what you do and with it the quality of your life increases dramatically."*

**- Eckhart Tolle**

This was one of the hardest chapters for me to write because it's the area that has been most difficult for me to grasp. I used to be pretty good about staying present in all conversations whether speaking on the phone or in person. But, thanks to the smart phone, being present is a struggle for me.

It seems we have been retrained in a negative way to avoid moments of silence. If we do experience a bit of stillness, it's instinctual to grab our phone and check it. But what are we checking for? Something that truly can't wait? We tell ourselves "no" and continue reaching for our phone an average of 344 times per day. We clearly feel like stillness is something to avoid, then we are told how great it is to multitask. Yes, multitasking has its benefits, but it doesn't allow us to stay in the moment or support concentration.

Eckhart Tolle says, "Our brains aren't meant to think, but answer. Thinking becomes our habit when we let outside influences and thoughts of the non-present occur." We are meant to respond and react to our present surroundings, but when we develop the habit of thinking, we tend to detach ourselves from the present and contemplate events that are not part of our current reality.

Our reality is the moment at hand. Allowing ourselves to sit with the present moment invites creativity to flourish. We enter a state of flow, and a perpetual state of peace and harmony.

Do you know the feeling when you're staring in awe at something so mesmerizing you lose track of everything else around you? I often get into this state when I am out in nature, staring at a beautiful landscape, or walking back home from the gym after a good workout. It's a time when I am not thinking of anything at all and I am at peace, with the world *around* me as well as the world *within* me. Being in the present moment, for me, comes with the feeling of being weightless. It's different though than a state of mindlessness.

Have you ever written down the date in January and you got the month and the day correct, but you filled in the incorrect year? If you tell me you've never made that mistake, either you a rare anomaly or you're full of shit. Why do so many of us make that mistake during the first month or two of each new year? We could chalk it up to habit and mindlessness since we've written down the previous year so many times. And this is probably the most accurate answer, however, what if it's also a reminder of how quickly time passes?

We remember certain days so clearly, weeks are slightly less clear, and months and years fly by in a blur. So does our time here on this planet. It seems like the older we get, the more time speeds up. This is not just because our days are so full that time goes by so quickly, it's because our minds are so full with unnecessary clutter that it gets harder and harder to stay fully engaged in the present moment.

We keep our minds busy worrying about what's coming up, or reflecting on past events that were significant to us, and it's easy to dismiss the present moment instead of letting it have its place in the sun. But to think we are guaranteed a future is naive and arrogant. How many people's lives have ended unexpectedly when no one ever saw it coming? We look at these instances as sad, but it's *really* sad if don't learn from them. When we're young, we think our lives will never end, or at least not so abruptly. But truly, none of us are given any guarantees.

The only moment that matters in this life is the current one. Nothing else truly exists. Not the past, nor the future. The past is made up of memories about *what* was and *how* it was, rather than what actually occurred in the present moment when you were there.

Have you ever had a discussion with a friend or sibling about a concert you both attended or an argument that occurred between you in the past? Your recollection and their recollection of those events may have similarities, but the details can differ greatly. Neither of you is 100 percent accurate in your recollection. The mind morphs events and manipulates them with each person's perspectives and emotions attached to those events. No matter how accurate your memory is, any past moment was not exactly as you remember it.

And the future? Please. The future is pure fiction and speculation of how we want things to go, or don't want things to go, or how we think things should go. But none of that ever lines up perfectly with how things actually go.

Ancient renowned philosopher and stoic, Seneca, says, "We suffer so much more in imagination that we do in reality." Think about instances when you were worried how things were going to go and they went amazingly well. Now, think about times when you thought, "This weekend is going to be *my* weekend." But then shit completely hit the fan. The future is not ours and never will be.

*Memento mori* means, "Remember you must die." I don't say this to scare you or to bring sadness. I only say this as a reminder that all you are guaranteed in this life is the present moment. So stop the needless suffering and remember, *memento mori*.

Learning to be present starts with simply pulling your mind back into the present moment every time it wanders. Breathe in and soak up the here and now. When we know how quickly time passes, why would we want to be in any other moment other than the one we're in right now?

In the television series, *Cosmos: A Spacetime Odyssey*, Neil deGrasse Tyson talks about a calendar, The Cosmic Calendar, that represents Earth's existence and, according to that calendar, all of our recorded history last 14 seconds! Yes, 14 seconds. Think about how long your lifespan will last, it's only blip in the vastness of time. It's up to us to make it count by creating a lasting impact.

I used to think I needed to achieve amazing feats in life in order to make an impact. But more and more I realize that working on myself and doing kind things for those around me can create an impact that lasts for generations. Simple things, like paying for the coffee of the person behind me in the drive-thru line can begin a chain reaction of kindness when that person pays for the next, and so on. Just as kindness can spread from one person to the next, it spreads from one generation to the next like a domino effect.

Kindness is a powerful way to make use of the present moment. And it spreads like wildfire because it *feels* good to *do* good. It not only affects the people receiving kindness, but also those who witness it. When others see kindness playing out, they feel it and get inspired to do the same. And you, of course, will always feel the love you give coming back to you.

So how do we stay in the present moment so we can spread this love? You wouldn't believe how easy it is. Every time you feel your thoughts drifting away from the *here and now*, catch yourself. Simply pay attention to what you are allowing to capture your attention. The next time you begin to daydream while someone is talking, or when you're writing an e-mail and the television sucks you in, recognize what's happening and boom, you are back in the present moment. Turn off the TV, put down your phone, and intentionally focus on the task at hand. The key to returning to the present is simply through the awareness that you are not in the moment.

In case you're still not convinced that living in the present moment is the way to go, or you're worried that it will be too difficult to retrain yourself, then I'll leave you with this. When you are living in the present moment, worries begin to fade away. You aren't giving energy to anything else except what you can hear, see, smell, taste, and touch.

Here's an example. Instead of mindlessly eating an apple while distracted by intrusive thoughts, feel its cool smoothness in your hand. Hear the crunch of your first bite. Smell the sweetness and taste the juicy tartness with every single chew. When you are thinking of nothing except how the apple is just what you need in this moment, your other "problems" vanish because you are no longer harping on them. You are truly enjoying where you are. You're dealing with the only task that matters which is savoring the apple. Deal with what you face in that immediate second and you realize that you don't really have a problem at all.

We call it "living in the present moment," not the present day, hour, or minute. It's this present second where the world slows down and you get clarity. You feel the wind at your back and the sun on your face. You listen to the world around you. You are connected. And that connection is powerful. When you're living in the moment, you develop the ability to focus on what needs your attention and a huge weight of imaginary suffering and worry is lifted off your shoulders.

Your time on this planet is limited. The present will soon be the past, so enjoy it while it lasts. Enjoy the here and now while you are here now.

# **TIPS:**

There is an app called the WeCroak app that reminds you five times a day that you will die with a daily quote. It's free and it's useful to cope with your mortality so you are reminded that wasting time wastes portions of your life away.

Whenever thoughts are racing through your mind, go back to your breath. Count each breath as you go. Paying attention to your breath will always take you back to the present moment.

Close your eyes and listen to your surroundings. Take in the birds, the wind, the cars passing by. They come and go just like the moment you are in. What emotions are you experiencing? What are you are sitting on? Feel how it supports you. What are you touching? How does it feel? How do *you* feel? Can you feel your heartbeat or the energy of your blood running through your veins? Take it all in, because this is what is currently happening. You are now back in the present.

Going back to your breath and paying attention to what you are sensing in this moment are grounding techniques. You can look up other techniques or create your own.

**Resources:**

The Power of Now, by Eckhart Tolle

WeCroak App

When Awareness Becomes Natural, by Sayadaw U Tejaniya

The Pocket, by Thich Nhat Hanh

# 13.
# A Healthy Routine

*"A disciplined mind brings happiness."*

## - The Buddha

One of the most important ways to improve your life and stay on the path of growth is to find a routine that works for you. You can still be a spontaneous creature if you wish, but without discipline you will be a feather in the wind, floating with no sense of direction.

A healthy morning routine helps you accomplish more at the very beginning of each day. It helps you focus. It gives you an extra boost of confidence to take on your day because you have already checked items off your list before you've had your breakfast. A healthy routine is all about putting you in a mindset to accomplish more without feeling the monotony you may fear when you hear the word "routine". As odd as it may sound, a healthy morning routine even starts with your bedtime routine because a good night's sleep helps you wake up early with the energy you need.

A healthy morning routine is all about getting your ass out of bed for starters. Marcus Aurelius wrote to himself about his struggles to get out of bed, "At dawn, when you have trouble getting out of bed, tell yourself: "I have to go to work — as a human being. What do I have to complain of, if I'm going to do what I was born for — the things I was brought into the world to do? Or is this what I was created for? To huddle under the blankets and stay warm? So you were born to feel 'nice'? Instead of doing things and experiencing them? Don't you see the plants, the birds, the ants and spiders and bees going about their individual tasks, putting the world in order, as best they can? And you're not willing to do your job as a human being? Why aren't you running to do what your nature demands?"

Marcus wrote this almost 2000 years ago. He was the emperor of Rome. He didn't have to do shit if he didn't want to. He made the choice of living a disciplined life which makes his words all the more profound. And yet he had the same problem most of us still have in the mornings. Our beds are nice and cozy and comfortable. It's tempting to stay under the covers, but so much of your life is wasted by being lazy. While getting enough rest is important, we aren't built to sleep our lives away. Get up, get out, and seize the day. Remember, growing and changing means getting uncomfortable.

It is much easier to get out of bed when you plan accordingly and get to bed at a reasonable hour. I'm not saying you can't have some late nights now and then. And if you're a night owl, you can adapt your morning routine to start later. But give yourself limits so you can have consistency. Both night owls and early morning folks can take advantage of the minimal distractions, whether at the ass crack of dawn or late-night witching hours.

I would highly recommend some type of meditation focused on your breathing or expressing gratitude simply for waking up. Allow your routine to begin in silence so you can be present with your thoughts. Surround yourself with whatever puts you in a mindset to let go and be free.

I'll give you an example of my routine, which is about an hour long in total. But before I get into that, I have one piece of advice: DO NOT USE YOUR PHONE FOR THE FIRST HOUR OF BEING AWAKE OR THE LAST HOUR BEFORE GOING TO BED. Don't check your texts, e-mail, or social media. They'll be fine going unanswered for an hour, and your mind will thank you. If, and this is a big *if*, you can be disciplined to use your phone for a meditation app or some type of tool for learning, I recommend turning the phone to focus mode.

I am a morning person. I built my morning routine based on what makes me feel good and what gets my head into a good place before I set out into the world. Having that positive foundation to start my day helps me tackle almost anything that comes my way. The best part is, I start my morning routine while laying in bed. I wake up, lie in bed, and do a 10-minute meditation. I either count my breaths up and down ( 1, 2, 3, 4, 5, 6, 7, 7, 6, 5, 4, 3, 2, 1) or I break my meditation into three parts. The counting helps me align my mind and body while also distracting me from racing thoughts that could overtake my peace. This 10-minute practice helps bring me to the present moment. If my mind wanders, and it does, I don't judge myself but simply go right back to counting. This method is one I learned from reading Wim Hof's, book *The Wim Hof Method*.

Breaking up my meditation into three parts offers some variety. I'll focus on my breathing, then visualize good thoughts and feelings, and then end by repeating a mantra. This exercise is something I incorporated from Jay Shetty's book, *Think Like a Monk*. But here is where the spontaneity can kick in. You can repeat whatever you're feeling in the moment. You can visualize whatever you are needing in the moment. Your needs from day to day can change, so variety helps you consistently attune yourself to whatever is helpful.

After my 10-minute meditation, I get up and go to my living room, where I do a short yoga session followed by a few rounds of Wim Hof breathing exercises. I then reward myself with a cup of hot tea while I journal. Within an hour, I have set my mind and body up for success. I have accomplished tasks within the first hour of being awake that will give me the momentum I need to tackle the rest of the day.

There are plenty of other options for how to start a helpful daily routine, but I highly encourage you to consider one that offers silence and solitude. So much of our days are go, go, go. It's a noisy, busy world we live in. And all that commotion can send our minds into all different directions. Starting your day off quietly and alone helps you become more self-aware. By having such a routine, the outside world seems to slow down so you can become more focused. You feel more grounded and can more easily step out into the world and take it on with the care and confidence you need.

# TIPS:

My morning routine has been influenced by countless books, people, TED Talks, and Youtube meditations. Feel free to explore and try different things to find what works best for you.

I suggest starting with YouTube. It's free and there are an abundance of choices for a variety of meditations. I discovered the Wim Hof Method from a book called *Breath*, by James Nestor. Wim Hof wrote his own book, *The Wim Hof Method* and he also has a website where you can learn the method for free. It has had an amazing effect on my life and I encourage you to investigate it for yourself.

Regardless of what you find that works best for you, always reward yourself at the end of your routine. A cup of coffee, tea, breakfast, or whatever tickles your fancy. When you first begin your routine it can be tough to continue, but while you're building this habit, the best way to motivate yourself is with that reward at the end. Once you repeat your routine consistently for awhile, you'll no longer need the reward and the routine will eventually *become* the reward. Before long, a healthy routine will become the sacred part of your day.

**Resources:**

The Wim Hof Method, by Wim Hof

Breath, by James Nestor

Meditations, by Marcus Aurelius

Think Like a Monk, by Jay Shetty

# 14.
# Chip Away



*"Set thy heart upon thy work, but never on its reward."*

**– The Bhagavad Gita**

From a young age, I've always wanted to finish tasks to feel that sense of accomplishment and move on to the next item on my list. The more I completed, the more successful I thought I was. And accomplishing projects is a great feat. But I was always left feeling unsatisfied, even after finishing a task. It wasn't until I started doing the work on myself that I realized why I felt unsatisfied. There were two reasons.

First, I wasn't tackling the most difficult of undertakings. Studies have shown that making progress on difficult tasks leads to a release of dopamine. But I wasn't challenging myself. I was only doing simple chores that I could complete quickly, so I never got that dopamine boost. I had set the bar too low so I could complete the task and pat myself on the back. I wasn't allowing myself to take on tasks that felt uncomfortable or required me to be vulnerable.

Secondly, and most importantly, I wasn't taking the time to enjoy the journey. I wasn't learning anything during the process because I was hurrying along to reach the final destination as fast as I could. But then I'd look back and realize I didn't complete most tasks correctly or to the best of my ability. I discovered that doing a hack job, with holes so big they are visible from outer space, is not genuinely satisfying.

I needed to learn how to enjoy each step of the process rather than focus only on the feeling of crossing the finish line. I needed to let my routine carry over into how I would achieve my goals.

Your healthy morning routine prepares you to take on the rest of your day, and once you've got a goal or an objective in mind, what do you have to do to get there? What are the steps you have to take? Plan out these steps, then forget about every single step except the one in front of you.

Imagine you're blindfolded and you're climbing a staircase. If you don't focus solely on the step you're taking, you're likely to fall. Concentrate on the task at hand, not the accolades and rewards you think will come with the end result.

James Clear's *Atomic Habits*, talks about how accomplishing the little things and building up "atomic habits" leads to big transformations. But you do the big work by focusing on the tiniest of details, improving in 1% increments. Focusing on the tiny step in front of you helps you build momentum for each successive step and completing a step creates a hit of dopamine. We feel that hit and it gives us more momentum.

Doing something huge and complex isn't necessary for creating something of significance. You can't drive a car before it's built. James Clear states, "If you can get better 1% every day for a year then you'll end up thirty-seven times better by the time you're done." The good atomic habits we develop, aren't usually seen immediately because they are so small, but they are all parts of the amazing car that is being assembled, and during the process it is momentum that will serve as fuel that will make the car go.

Focusing heavily on the finish line is one of the biggest reasons why many people fail to reach their goals. They get so excited that they skip steps and completely screw up their objectives. They can't wait to tell everyone about their brilliant idea, but then forget to do any of the behind-the-scenes work it takes to get there.

I recall when I first moved out to Los Angeles, I wrote a script with my best friend and writing partner at the time. This story was essentially poking fun at the whole Hollywood process. We thought it was THE SHIT! In reality, it *was* shit and it was offensive to people who had years and years invested in the industry. When we sent our "masterpiece" out to our contacts, we heard nothing but crickets.

Our script wasn't ready and neither were we. But we were so excited that we rushed it out the door. None of those contacts ever took our calls again, because we didn't put our best foot forward. We didn't pay attention to the preparation and details necessary for the process.

There is no short cut for doing the work. The tasks and steps can change over the course of your journey, and they should. Just remain patient. While you're going through the development process, problem areas can and will present themselves. When they do, you can alter your steps and account for the problem areas. This process will produce a better end result if you're not skipping those essential learning opportunities. If you wait until the end of any big goal to address problems, you may discover they are harder (or even impossible) to resolve. So address problems sooner rather than later. Take your time and take things step-by-step. If you're not about doing the work properly, maybe this idea doesn't suit you in the first place.

Having trouble getting excited about the actual process of obtaining a goal is why so many large or difficult goals are never accomplished. But the notoriety, the exposure, the fame doesn't come without putting in the work and even learning to enjoy the process. I've seen this eagerness for the end result play out so many times living in Los Angeles and working in the film industry. Some folks move out to LA and jump into the Hollywood scene, without learning the skills necessary for success in the entertainment business. They're here, not because they love the art of acting or filmmaking, but because they want the fame that comes along with it. If you aren't passionate about the process and the work that it takes to accomplish your goal, then it's time to move on and find a goal that really lights that fire within you.

It's okay if the path you choose changes, and it most likely will. There is no right or wrong path to blazing our unique trail. And it is so important to pay attention when the road you're on no longer feels in sync with who you are. Maybe you went into the process excited and motivated, but now the work you're doing just doesn't seem worthy of your time. When that happens, you can simply adjust your course.

We are human. Our tastes and interests change. There was a time when all I ever wanted to do was produce films and television programs. I still enjoy that work, but my passions have shifted. When I realized I didn't enjoy the process as much as I used to, I asked myself what it was about film that brought me joy in the first place. Then I thought about how I might take that element and do it elsewhere. When I asked myself, "What is my superpower and how can I use it best?" I thought about how much I enjoy growing and inspiring others to grow. So I altered my path.

It's a powerful thing to recognize when the sails are still blowing you in the direction of your current goal and to adjust your course if the winds have shifted. After doing that, I now put most of my time and energy on this objective of doing what I most enjoy. My main goal now is to make the world a better place.

When you focus on the end result, it's easy to get overwhelmed at how far you have to go. You tend to become dejected when your goal doesn't come to fruition quickly. You might even feel like a failure before you start because it feels too hard, especially if you start doubting that you'll never get there.

I have news for you, it will be hard. It's going to drive you bonkers from time to time. You're going to question whether or not you are good enough and whether or not accomplishing this goal is going to be worth all the effort. Anyone who has ever accomplished anything has felt this way at some point. This is all normal.

The way to calm your mind is by not hyper-focusing on the big picture. It's okay to have it in the background and out of focus. What needs to be fully in focus is the task right in front of you. When I wrote this book I didn't just sit down in one sitting and type it all out. I had to write it in stages. I had to build it piece by piece, page by page. I had to take all that I have read from other sources, what I've read from my own journals, along with my own experiences, and build it word by word.

Whatever you are trying to accomplish will get done if you chip away. Chop that wood and the tree will eventually come down. Just focus on the step at hand. Then work your way to the next one, then the next one. Before you know it, you start gaining momentum. Then keep chugging along and eventually... boom! You have reached your goal. And once you have crossed the finish line, I'll bet you're going to feel satisfaction like you've never felt before. Who knows, when you finally finish, maybe meeting your big goal will inspire a new goal or project.

As you complete each task, step-by-step, celebrate the little wins. Celebrate that first step being completed. Then the second step. Celebrate the amazing revelation that challenges bring so you can fix a potential problem BEFORE it causes trouble. This is how you can enjoy the journey of your goal and not just the end game.

## TIPS:

Write down a goal that you wish to accomplish. Then, on a dry erase board or paper <u>with</u> <u>pencil</u>, write down all of the steps that need to be accomplished to achieve that goal. Next, cover the dry eraser board or list with another piece of paper which covers everything except task number one. Keep every step except the first covered until it is done, then uncover the next step and begin to work on it. Proceed like this until you've met your goal so you stay focused and present for each step.

Try using the Endowed Progress Effect. I'll explain. You have two drinking cups, one that is filled with the number of paper clips that are equal to the number of tasks on your list; and the other cup is empty. Each time you complete a task on your list, move a paperclip from one cup to the other. Then move onto the next task and move another paper clip over after it has been completed. Keep doing this until the tasks are done and the paperclips have all been transferred. This method is scientifically proven to increase the perceived value of each task. You will feel a deep sense of accomplishment and joy during the process. And, when you feel more accomplished you are more likely to keep doing the little tasks that allow you to move to the next step towards reaching your goal.

**Resources:**

*Atomic Habits,* by James Clear

# 15.
# Be Empathetic

————◆————

*"Wherever there is a human being, there is an opportunity for kindness."*

**- Seneca**

The smartest person in the room isn't necessarily the most well-read, or the one with the highest SAT scores, but rather the person with the most empathy, because that person is able to see the world from others' viewpoints. It's easy to have empathy for someone you like and agree with, but it can be difficult to have empathy with those who don't see eye to eye with you.

Developing greater empathy requires engaging with people who aren't exactly like you. It requires being open and listening. Remember to think like a scientist. The goal is not to change your mind about how you think or to change others' minds. Empathy is about gaining an understanding of another person's thinking and where they are coming from. So often we see the people as a "finished product" because we only see them as they are now, standing in front of us, but we forget about the process that brought them where they are. We don't realize all of the trials and tribulations that have made them who they are in the present moment.

Daryl Davis, a jazz musician turned activist, just so happened to be playing a venue one night when his music impressed a particular guest. Between musical sets, that guest walked up to Daryl and told him, "That's the first time I heard a black man play like Jerry Lee Lewis." Daryl tried to explain the black origin of the music, but the man didn't believe Daryl. He decided to buy Daryl a drink, and this drink was going to be his first drink with a black man. Daryl was curious and he asked why that was? This audience member explained that he was an active member of the Ku Klux Klan.

Daryl had experienced racism since he was a kid and recalled the first time he noticed it when he was just 10 years old. He had always wondered, "How can someone hate me when they don't even know me?" Daryl had decided to interview Klan leaders across the country and discover where their disdain for black people came from, then he would write a book about it, *Klan-destine*. So, Daryl convinced this guest at his concert to give him the contact info for the Imperial Wizard, the leader of his Klan, so he could finally seek an answer to his big question.

The Klan leader's name was Roger Kelly. When Daryl and Roger met, Roger had no idea Daryl was black. Roger and his bodyguards were shocked. Roger agreed to be interviewed, but he was sure to let Daryl know how he was inferior to him because of the color of his skin. During the interview there was a crackling noise that startled the room. Daryl and Roger each thought the other was responsible for this noise. They were both afraid, but soon realized the noise was ice sliding down a bucket containing sodas. Once they came to this realization, they started laughing at how they were scared of something so innocent just because it was a noise they didn't understand.

Daryl used this example to explain how ignorance breeds fear, and how fear breeds hatred, then eventually destruction. I'd have to agree with him. I also believe that when you have empathy, you open yourself up to greater understanding.

Roger and Daryl continued these interviews over a period of time and would often have dinner and lunch together. After a couple of years of knowing each other, Roger invited Daryl to his home and eventually to the Klan rallies. They developed an extremely unexpected friendship. Daryl gained Roger's respect and vice versa because they were both able sit down and listen to one another. They didn't have to agree, but they sought to understand where each other was coming from and respected the other's perspective. As a result, Roger began to question his beliefs and eventually renounced the Klan and gave Daryl his robe and hood as a token of gratitude.

How did Daryl accomplish this monumental moment? It wasn't by chastising this guy or telling him how wrong his viewpoint was. No, Daryl simply asked him questions. He investigated. He set out to understand the process that led this man to hate Daryl and all black people without reasoning. Daryl approached it in an empathetic way rather than an egotistical tone that is so easy to use when we believe "we are right and they are wrong!"

I'm sure we all have countless examples of times when we ignored advice or another's viewpoint because they were jamming it down our throats. No one learns anything this way and we aren't changing anyone's mind. We all discover new perspectives in our own time and our own way. But when we ask others and ourselves the tough questions in a gentle manner, we create opportunities for ourselves and others to discover answers.

Lessons involving our character are rarely discovered until we do the discovering ourselves. Others can point us in the right direction, and even nudge us a little. But if they direct us or, even worse, attempt to force their perspectives on us, we usually don't pick up what they're puttin' down.

Daryl and Roger genuinely got to know each other and, by doing so, they began to understand one another, Roger discovered that his ideologies were not true to who he was anymore. He realized that hating a man when you don't even know him wasn't how he wanted to live his life. Daryl eliminated Roger's fear, by showing that he, too, is a person worthy of respect. We are always so fearful of what we don't know, because it's unfamiliar. And when things are unfamiliar, our minds race with the possibilities of what could happen and we rush to make our thoughts feel more familiar.

Daryl opened up his heart and allowed Roger to let down his guard. Through the power of listening, questioning, and choosing compassion, Daryl gained a deep understanding of the way Roger had come to his early conclusions. Daryl soon realized that fear was the driving force behind Roger's hate for people he didn't know. This willingness to investigate and to help someone discover themselves all came from Daryl's empathy for a complete stranger who hated him.

This former Klan wizard, and now countless others, have turned in their robes and denounced the Klan. Daryl had no obligation to assist Roger or anyone else on their journey of growth. This wasn't his responsibility, nor is it your job either to engage in similar situations. But it is amazing what happens when we search for empathy and find it.

Daryl's questions and friendship with a stranger not only benefited Roger, but Daryl ended up making a new friend in the process. It took a wise person to keep his cool and remain open-hearted with someone who outright hated him. But by doing so, he opened up doors he may never have known existed, and showed us all what is possible when we learn to be empathetic.

We all know the saying to "put yourself in their shoes." But we have to do more than that to truly understand someone. We have to feel what they feel, and imagine a lifetime of choices that got them to where and who they are today. And when we ask them questions, they can better understand themselves, too.

Think about how often we overlook all that has brought us to where we are now. We have to take a trip down memory lane to see how our decisions have resulted in certain outcomes, and now those outcomes led to the next choice, and the next until we reached the point where we are now.

When I look at my life, I see myself in LA for one day, then Wisconsin, then Indiana and back to LA. What led me to each of those places? How was my life affected by my decisions? What did I learn in each place? Looking at my own story and seeing how I got to where I am makes it easier for me to develop empathy for others because I have become more aware that others have a story as well.

The same is true for all of us. When we recognize our own story and respect it, we can look at others and do the same. Rather than write them off because they are a dick right now, maybe we can see them with more kindness and less judgement. Maybe we can listen more and ask questions that lead to greater understanding and, in turn, greater empathy. By learning to become empathetic, we can all become more like Daryl and help someone alter their own path, in addition to our own.

Empathy is quite possibly the most underrated trait in all of creation because it leads us on the path to discovering true connection with others. When we have empathy, we see the world from multiple perspectives and have the opportunity to question our beliefs about the way things are and always have been. We begin to develop a different palate. We begin to see how this part of town may not be so kind to someone else, or why traditions that seems so silly to one person means so much to others. We get a glimpse of how something that is so easy or so hard for us is a completely different experience for someone else. True knowledge starts with empathy because empathy is about understanding. Understanding fosters love, and there is no greater knowledge available to us than love.

## TIPS:

Look up some of the most vilified people in the world. Now pick one of them and find as much information about their lives as you can. How did they become this way? Did they have something traumatic happen to them that set them on this path? What was the process that made them the people they became?

If you are having difficulties with empathizing with someone, imagine them as a child or a teenager. Do you know what their life has been like? Who were they? Why might they have become the person they are today? Think of how you felt as a teen and the times you felt ostracized or alone. They may still be feeling that now. What might it look like to give them the benefit of the doubt?

**Resources:**

*Greenlights* by Matthew McConaughey

# 16.
# Dust Yourself Off
# and Try Again

*"Failure is success in progress."*

**- Albert Einstein**

This guide isn't just here to make you feel good. That is not the goal. The goal is to become self-aware, to keep improving, and to always keep moving forward, even when you fall a couple steps back.

Change isn't going to happen overnight, and you are undoubtedly going to fail at times. You'll wonder if you've got what it takes to change. You will face doubts, but don't give up. You are not alone. Everyone experiences doubts in our abilities and we all question whether or not we are good enough from time to time. Doubts aren't a bad thing. They even help us, by bringing up questions we need to ask ourselves.

Rather than giving in to doubts, observe them and seek to understand why they are there in the first place. Just don't let them become a backseat driver. Know that perseverance will be the thing that gets you results, and that you are never really finished growing until you're six feet under. Just keep going.

I struggled with doubts writing this book. So many times I wondered what the hell I was doing and if I was good enough to write it. Am I experienced enough? Can someone actually find value in this?

This book is me dusting myself off and trying again. So much of what you have read has come from my journal entries, my thoughts, and my pain. I wrote all of this down to remind myself that I have overcome trials, that I have faced adversity, and I am still here. It has taken me years and years to get to where I am now and I still need to review the contents of these pages to pick myself up when I falter. I now experience more joy than ever, but I still feel pain and sorrow. Difficulties are never going to go away, but I know how to deal with them now. I know how to accept *what is*.

Navy Seals do a training exercise called *drown proofing*, where they are dropped in a pool with their hands and feet tied. They are told they need to survive in the water for 5 minutes. 70-85% of Navy Seals fail at this exercise. Most people squirm and struggle to keep their heads above water and they panic. But the ones that complete the task successfully? Well, they don't struggle, but instead let themselves hit the bottom of the pool and kick off the pool floor to rise above the water to take a breath. They repeat this exercise until the 5 minutes are up. They don't fight the restraints, they don't attempt to free themselves, but they stay calm knowing they can keep bouncing back until they're finally out of the water. Similarly, we can't fight life when we are sinking, we have to find a way to keep bouncing back.

We all experience a full spectrum of emotions, and that is a good thing. When we feel sadness, anger, and discouragement, these emotions can actually guide us and help us appreciate joy, love, and the highs of life. Think about it. Would you know what joy is if you never felt sadness? If you were always joyful would you appreciate the feeling or would you take it for granted because you'd expect to always feel this way?

Failing is normal. It is necessary for growth. Don't run from pain and struggles. Face them knowing that you *can* and *will* come back stronger from missteps. You are the only person who can truly keep you down.

Michael Jordan's famous quote says, "I've lost almost 300 games. Twenty-six times I've been trusted to take the game winning shot and missed. I've failed over and over and over again in life and that's why I succeed."

The same is true for any leader, athlete, and champion. The biggest difference between winners and those who are defeated has to do with the mindset of bouncing back and learning from mistakes.

We have all felt hurt and we will feel it again. We've all said the wrong thing at the wrong time. We've all had bad moments when we have been complete assholes. We will continue to have those moments, yet with practice and growth we don't have to let our reactions spill onto others nor do we need to let difficult moments turn into bad days.

As you start becoming more aware of the behaviors you want to change, you won't be as likely to continue that behavior.

You'll feel whatever you are feeling and then move on. You'll notice whenever something you are doing doesn't seem to align with who you are anymore. Then, instead of beating yourself up for setbacks or mistakes, you'll recognize that icky feeling and move forward wiser and stronger.

Even self-awareness and growth will not make any of us invincible to our faults. Learning, growing, and discovering more about ourselves helps us become aware of new areas we need to work on. Even still, old problem areas tend to make a comeback now and then. Just when we think we have one area fixed, we might falter in another area. That's just part of being a human being.

Alcoholics who haven't had a drink in years still call themselves alcoholics. Anyone who has overcome demons before remains susceptible to face them again. Just know that it's how you bounce back that matters. You can learn from any obstacle you face, even if it's self-inflicted. *Especially* when it's self-inflicted.

Be gentle with yourself on your journey to greater self-awareness. Even the people you admire most in the world have suffered from mess-ups and imposter syndrome from time to time. They still mess up, but they also learn from their messes and clean them up afterward. You can and will do the same. Failure is never final.

There will be some failures that are your own fault and those that are out of your control. It is important to distinguish one from the other and equally important to forgive yourself for each and to move on. The love and patience you show yourself will flow to those who surround you as well.

# **TIPS:**

Take yourself out on a date every now and then. Go see a movie, go out to dinner, do whatever you love the most and do it alone. You deserve it.

Doubts and failures are a normal part of our evolution process. Doubts are a way our brains try to pull us back to the comfort zone that has become so ingrained in our daily lives. Doubts relentlessly strive to keep us in a state of perpetual ease. Don't give in to these voices. They are the voices of regression and fear, but sometimes they have something we can learn from. They are never going to fully go away. They are part of you and it's a good time to get to know them without letting them be in the driver's seat.

# PART IV:
## The Why

# 17.
# The Why


*"Whatever we do to the web, we do to ourselves. All things are bound together. All things connect."*

**- Chief Seattle, Duwamish Tribe**

I started this book with an introduction admitting to you that I am no expert. I told you that I believe change occurs from within and when we change ourselves, we change the world. Now, of course, I am going to tell you *why*. After all, I've encouraged you throughout this guide to always ask *why*.

I don't claim to have all the answers to the world and its problems. I don't know the true meaning of humanity's existence, but based on my experiences and the incredible spiritual mentors I respect, I have come to an understanding that I want to pass along for your consideration. I had my doubts about whether or not to share this, just like I had my doubts about being qualified to write this guide. But here it goes.

Each chapter of this guide begins with a quote by a philosopher, messiah, genius, or whatever you would like to call these incredible individuals. For the sake of simplicity, I'll refer to them as philosophers here. And these philosophers all have one thing in common: No matter what the religion or following that proceeded them, no matter what era they existed within, no matter what stories have led to their legacy, they all believed in being kind to one another and being compassionate. They all believed that love, is what connects us all.

When we ask for guidance from a higher power, we are acknowledging the connection through which we all live and breathe. We are letting go of the idea that we are alone and in control over our lives, and we are allowing our souls to tap into a source that is far bigger and deeper than we can fathom. Even after our physical bodies cease to exist, we are forever part of this much larger reality. And love is at the heart of it all.

In Russell Brand's book, *Revelation,* he puts so eloquently what I have sensed throughout my whole life: "That we are awareness experiencing temporary form."

Our souls are riding along in these vehicles called our bodies, and eventually our vehicles will break down and enter the junkyard, but the awareness doesn't go away. Our souls don't go down with the ship. It's scientifically proven that energy cannot be destroyed, and we are made of energy.

So why did all of these great philosophers believe that we should be kind to one another and radiate love? Because they believed or knew that we are all part of a great oneness. That together we form Voltron or Captain Planet or whatever nerdy analogy floats your boat. We are part of a collective. We are all connected energy and the *We* I am talking about is all that surrounds us. The air we breathe, the water we drink, and the life we share this planet with are all connected to us. Brand goes on further to say, "Love is the awareness of absolute union, the ulterior reality beneath apparent separation."

Why does it feel so good to help others? Why can we see and feel the pain inflicted on others even when we are the ones inflicting that pain? Why do we feel a calm with the sounds of nature even when they are coming from our phone's speakers? Maybe it's because we all feel that connectedness that we long for.

Together our energies can achieve another level. The whole is greater than the sum of its parts. On the flip side, when we see harm done to another living being, we feel that pain to some degree. We feel an injustice has been done. We hurt because we are one with the victim who has this pain inflicted upon them. Every attack on our fellow beings and the world around us is felt within us.

So if the harm and love we all feel is connected then the love we give ourselves is felt by others, too. When we're chipping away and constantly evolving every day, that is a result of the love we have for ourselves and in essence reflects love for the whole.

I truly believe that once you're consistently chipping away at it, you will love the process of evolving, because you will see your results by the love and compassion you pass on to others.

The joy that filled my life wasn't the result of some breakthrough or one big "aha!" moment. It started when I began to love the process of growing. When an obstacle presented itself and I no longer got angry or dejected, I really started to feel the shift in my life. I was excited to take on the challenge. That's what evolving is all about, it's about chipping away and knowing that every swing of the axe is progress, and that progress brings the fulfillment we're after.

I mentioned in Chapter 11: Beliefs and Your Character, that I believe the journey we are on is the discovery of who we were before society got its hands on us. Now I'll take it a step further, because again, we should be the scientist and question everything while being open to relearning things.

What if the journey we are on is about the discovery of who we were before we even entered this world? What if our mission in life is a journey meant to strengthen and challenge our connection to the whole? And in order to strengthen that connection to *all that is*, we must strengthen it within ourselves, individually. Then we can help one another do the same. As we reach our higher selves, we discover that we are beautiful the way we are; an intricate and necessary part of the whole. Transformation begins within us and, if we are all doing our part, we grow stronger, together.

So I'll end this book with the way we started which is by asking you a few questions. Why are you here? How are you going to start changing your life? What do you truly enjoy doing? How can you use your gifts to uplift others and to shine more light on the world that surrounds you?

We don't have to do amazing feats to have an impact. We can start with being more kind to our fellow beings. The smallest acts seem to have the greatest effect, beginning with the work you do on yourself. By doing that work, individuals create ripples in the water, and when we are all making ripples, we can make giant waves that shape the world in the most beautiful and powerful ways.

# Tips:

Only you can know your *why*. Dig deep and do some soul searching. Take time alone for yourself and be present. Find calm in the quiet and ask why? Journal whatever comes up. Continue to write down your questions, milestones, and lessons learned in the days, months, and years to come.

**Resources:**

*Revelation,* by Russell Brand

*The Celestine Prophecy,* by James Redfield

# Resources

www.ingramcontent.com/pod-product-compliance
Lightning Source LLC
Chambersburg PA
CBHW050733150726
48196CB00038B/905/J